A Journey Through The Psalms

Reflections For Worried Hearts And Troubled Times

Preaching The Psalms
Cycles A, B, C

Schuyler Rhodes

CSS Publishing Company, Inc., Lima, Ohio

Scripture quotations are from the New Revised Standard Version of the Bible, copyright
1989 by the Division of Christian Education of the National Council of the Churches of
Christ in the USA. Used by permission.

This material first appeared in issues of *Emphasis* from 2005-2007. Copyright owned by
CSS Publishing Company, Inc.

Library of Congress Cataloging-in-Publication Data

Rhodes, Schuyler, 1953-
    A journey through the Psalms : reflections for worried hearts and troubled times :
preaching the Psalms, Cycles A, B, C / Schuyler Rhodes.
        p. cm.
    "This material first appeared in issues of Emphasis from 2005-2007"—T.p. verso
Includes index.
ISBN-13: 978-0-7880-2627-0 (perfect bound : alk. paper)
ISBN-10: 0-7880-2627-5 (perfect bound : alk. paper)
1. Bible. O.T. Psalms—Meditations. 2. Common lectionary (1992). I. Title.

BS1430.54.R46 2009
223'.207—dc22

2009005493

For more information about CSS Publishing Company resources, visit our website at
www.csspub.com or email us at csr@csspub.com or call (800) 241-4056.

Cover design by Barbara Spencer
ISBN-13: 978-0-7880-2627-0
ISBN-10: 0-7880-2627-5
PRINTED IN USA

*This book is dedicated
with a grateful heart
to Lisa Quoresimo,
my spouse,
my partner,
and my beloved companion
on this journey.*

Table Of Contents

The following psalms do not appear in the Revised Common Lectionary: 3, 6-7, 10-12, 18, 21, 28, 35, 38-39, 55-61, 64, 87-88, 94, 101-102, 108-109, 115, 117, 120-121, 129, 134-135, and 140-142.

These writings were originally assigned for the *Emphasis* preaching magazine and were date specific. Some psalms were never assigned.   R. K. Allen, Managing Editor

Introduction

As a people, we are not given over much to introspection or reflection. In the rush and bustle to accomplish and achieve we rarely pause to ponder the path on which we have embarked. Indeed, if asked where we were headed in such a hurry, the response would more likely be a befuddled glance backward as we quickened our pace and moved along the road to an unknown and unexamined destination.

In these times of uncertainty and economic gloom the frenzied pace quickens. It brings to mind the fabled White Rabbit of *Alice in Wonderland* fame — always in a rush to go nowhere in particular. He had no time to stop, no time to look left or right, and certainly no time for introspection or self-examination. It's as though the patterns of our lives bespeak the fear that our mouths rarely mention.

For people of faith, however, reflection is important. As an imperfect people pursuing the perfect wonder of God, we require frequent pauses for rest and reflection so that we can take the opportunity to examine the terrain and think about the direction we're headed. A person of faith takes the time to examine motive and intent. A person of faith, like a good driver on the highway, looks in all directions to try and avoid collisions. Finally, a person of faith creates moments for listening. So often our relationship with God is a one-way street of petitionary prayer. It is, we must admit, too much about our needs and desires. A time, therefore, when the mind and the mouth are shut down, is a space where God's voice just might get a word in edgewise.

The psalms are just the ticket for such sacred pauses. They are wonderful vehicles for reflection and prayer. Each one emerges from the ancient and ongoing human struggle to relate to a creating and liberating God. Each one greets the reader with an invitation to enter into a prayerful dialogue with the holy. Through the psalms we walk the gambit of both sacred and secular reality. From shouts and singing to dancing, weeping, and moaning, the psalms accompany us on our walk of faith. Together they constitute a series of love letters to God; poems of wonder and hope. They are the sung and sighed utterances of ancestors who walk with us still.

Each person who engages the psalms will find some different ore to be mined. Some will find a sympathetic companion. Others will find challenge, still others will discover comfort. A reflective few will stumble headlong into a powerful new experience of the holy.

By way of confession, the offerings in this collection are the reflections of a preacher. The preacher's heart leans, from both habit and passion, into what might be shared. It veers into unpacking God's word as a communal rather than individual exercise. So it is that these few words are the efforts of one miner to find a special and deeply personal ore that cannot remain as such.

These musings are part of a dialogue with the text. There are times when it's a lover's quarrel. There are moments when it is an astounded guffaw, and there a few flashes of anger and inability to comprehend a God such as ours. Faith, it turns out, has little to do with actual understanding.

No matter how the written word is offered, it is always filtered through those who pick up the book to read. To each of you who do me this honor, I can only attest to the authenticity contained herein. No matter what path is taken or perspective explored, it is at least the honest jottings of a parish pastor.

It's my profound hope that you discover some joy, some awe, and even a chuckle or two in the reading. Whatever is found, this space for reflection is offered humbly.

Schuyler Rhodes

Psalm 1

It would be an easy thing to read through this psalm and nod in assent before moving on to the next. It all seems pretty obvious. "Happy are those who do not follow the advice of the wicked, or take the path that sinners tread...." It is tantamount to what the young people refer to as a "no-brainer." Much of this bad advice could be avoided by turning off our televisions. And the sinner's well-worn walkways? They too seem fairly apparent. Yet somehow they continue to be well worn.

Today it is the seat of the scoffers that merits attention. Scoffing, or as the King James Bible has it, being "scornful," is considered high sport these days. From a burgeoning host of television shows where people are scorned and insulted in public, to a peanut gallery of scoffers who take delight in deriding most anything that tries to rise up or to be even slightly noble, it is ubiquitous. Cynicism is in fashion. There can be no heroes anymore. Everyone is under the microscope, and any flaws that are found are hoisted up as proof of perfidy.

Heroes like Martin Luther King Jr., Mahatma Gandhi, Eleanor Roosevelt, and many, many more have been examined and found wanting in their humanness. The role of scorn and derision has become so central in our culture that many who would take a stand or assume the mantle of leadership decline to do so. Shoulders shrug and a sharp breath escapes, "Who needs it?"

The psalm is clear and hits at a stark truth. "Happy, very happy, is the one who does not sit in the seat of the scoffers...." It follows then, that blessings and happiness are not a part of the vernacular of scorn.

Perhaps the most distressing piece of all this is the fact that our churches are not immune. In some places, the pews where we worship have become the "seats of the scoffers."

In this maelstrom of negative energy, the voice of the holy calls to those of us who call ourselves Christians. Can we, who must navigate the currents and eddies of this culture, create a true sanctuary in our church? Can we, who claim Christ as Lord, reclaim Christian community as a place where people are truly safe?

Dare we unseat the scoffers? Dare we make it clear that in our churches it is imperative that each person be physically, emotionally, and spiritually safe? Dare we stand together to create a community where everyone is welcome, and everyone is respected?

The answer, coming from Jesus who went before us is, "Yes. Yes. In fact, I double dare you."

Psalm 1

This psalm could have been written yesterday! It is striking in its contemporaneous feel. Think about it. Today the airwaves are full of those who would offer advice. From familiar newspaper advice columns to the proliferation of so-called professionals who offer advice on everything from dating to careers to investing and back again, everyone wants to get in on the act. Moreover, the media and its corporate handlers offer the seductive sinner's path to anyone who is willing to take the hike. Violence is chic, infidelity is standard, and religion is a joke. The "scoffer's seat" is held up as an ideal place to be in this day of cynical derision and near universal lack of trust. It is a desolate and joyless landscape, indeed.

Thus it is that this psalm offers a way out. Those who refuse the addled advice of commerce-driven talking heads are more likely to find happiness. Those who resist the manifold temptations to walk the paths that sinners tread, similarly have access to happiness.

And the scoffers? How can there be joy in the process of tearing down others? How can there be happiness in positioning oneself as an adversary to anything and everyone that comes along with a new idea or a creative option? Cynicism may be trendy, but it is devoid of happiness except for a sneering kind of *schadenfreude* that is best left on the shelf next to the latest tabloid.

Real happiness comes in the clarity that emerges from a community of faith that is rooted in God. Like a tree next to a river, such a people do not thirst or grow weary. Instead, as nourished and connected people, they grow and flourish in the ways of trust, hope, and new beginnings.

Creating such communities within our churches is one of the most critical callings of the church today. In a world of vaunted and narcissistic individualism, the caring voice of community beckons. In a time when noble and good efforts are ridiculed as silly and useless in the so-called "real world," the idealism of Christian community stands as an island in the storm. In the midst of a runaway, consumerist culture where feelings and instincts are numbed by the ever-present pressure to acquire more and more, God's yearning reaches out to awaken us.

Yes, indeed. This psalm could have been written yesterday. Perhaps, today a new psalm might emerge celebrating the joy of those who have staked their claim in loving, authentic Christian community.

Psalm 2

There is an old preacher's joke that asks the question, "How do you make God laugh?" The answer that follows quickly is short and to the point — "Make plans." Anyone who has had their carefully laid plans foiled by fate can attest to the truth contained in this joke. From vacations to careers to families, relationships and beyond, the words of old rock-and-roller, John Lennon, bear the reality that life is something that happens while you're busy making plans.

The message is clear. Our plans and strategies amount to little in the wake of life's exegencies. That this is true on an individual level seems clear enough, but it is to those who plan and "conspire" in the seats of power that this psalm addresses itself. From the days of King David right on through to the moment of this writing, it has ever been the same with kings and presidents, dictators and leaders. Those who find themselves in power inevitably find themselves wound up in plots and conspiracies that aim at confounding the purposes of God. Those in power plot and conspire to oppress workers and those who live on the land. It has been thus for millennia. Perhaps 1 Samuel puts it best as the people of Israel clamor for a king and God explains the ways of the king.

These will be the ways of the king who will reign over you: he will take your sons and appoint them to his chariots and to be his horsemen, and to run before his chariots; and he will appoint for himself commanders of thousands and commanders of fifties, and some to plow his ground and to reap his harvest, and to make his implements of war and the equipment of his chariots. He will take your daughters to be perfumers and cooks and bakers. He will take the best of your fields and vineyards and olive orchards and give them to his courtiers. He will take one-tenth of your grain and of your vineyards and give it to his officers and his courtiers. He will take your male and female slaves, and the best of your cattle and donkeys, and put them to his work. He will take one-tenth of your flocks, and you shall be his slaves. And in that day you will cry out because of your king, whom you have chosen for yourselves; but the Lord will not answer you in that day. — 1 Samuel 8:11-18*

Though we passed the one-tenth mark long ago in terms of what today's kings take, the essence and truth ring with clarity down the centuries. But still, from the White House to the Kremlin; from Paris to Managua and back they continue to plot and conspire. And God? God continues to laugh.

Psalm 4

A great piece of advice was once offered by a sage, elder pastor. "It's okay," he said, "even necessary, to acknowledge our feelings and to work through them. But it is unwise, especially when we are angry or upset, to act out of those emotions." This one hits close to home. Over more than two decades in the pastorate, this writer has witnessed the destruction and even death caused by people who have made decisions or taken actions when they are in the throes of anger or beset by depression.

"When you are disturbed, do not sin" (v. 4).

There are many times in the course of our days that we find ourselves caught in the snares of anger. There are times, too, when the dark sides of our souls hold sway and we are caught in the maze of depression. Not to be flip, but this is life. The trick, for so many of us, is not so much to avoid these circumstances, but to be able to navigate the shoals of our emotional landscape without hurting ourselves or others in the process. In other words, we need to learn not to sin when we are "disturbed."

The writer of this psalm seems to have stumbled upon something here. He is clearly disturbed. But he turns to a God who cuts him some slack. "You gave me room when I was in distress." God is a good place for us to go when life seizes us in this way. If we must rail against our fate, shake our fists in anger, then God — it seems — can take it.

"God is a shield for all those who take refuge in him" (2 Samuel 22:31). The old Luther hymn comes to mind here. "A mighty fortress is our God...." In a time when people are widely encouraged to let it all out, it can be easy to lose track of the need for self-control and restraint. Indeed, it's possible to work through feelings in a healthy way without spewing the baggage of those emotions on unsuspecting and innocent bystanders. And for us, this avenue lies in taking our anger, our depression, our "disturbed" hearts to God. In prayer, in discernment, in quiet time with our Savior, it is possible to sort out the storms that beset our hearts. In the quiet space we take to be alone with God, we can separate out our feelings from the decisions we make and the actions we take.

Will we still need the help of our pastors, of therapists, and of other people whose work is centered in helping us in these arenas? Certainly. But do we need God in these moments as well? Absolutely. Perhaps, as we move through the rocky paths that come to us on our journey, we will learn how to reach for God while we seek the help we need from those God has placed in our path.

Psalm 5:1-8

Everyone knows what it's like to surrender in a long, collapsing sigh. There is no one who has lived who cannot summon up memories of times when adversaries or enemies seemed to be everywhere. Such struggles sap the soul and often leave us feeling as though there are no options; no place left to turn. It is this sense of powerlessness that comes through this psalm.

"Give heed to my sighing. Listen to the sound of my cry...." What poignant scenes enter the mind as the imagination conjures up the sounds of sighs and sobs, the spirit of despair.

Yet, it turns out that there is one place left to turn. There is one court of last resort, even when a host of enemies surrounds and threatens, there is one who does not fade away. God's faithfulness stands with arms outstretched to all generations. God's abundant and steadfast love does not go away.

It is this abundance that is nearly impossible to grasp. In a world of limitations where it seems that there is never enough, the notion of abundance feels foreign, strange. We learn through thorough acculturation that there is never enough love, never enough power, never enough hope, never enough ... stuff; and so our lives become a competitive struggle to gain and maintain a piece of the pie.

But in God there is abundance. That is to say, there is not merely enough to go around; there is more than plenty for everyone.

So it is that in desperation, when all else fails, we turn to God and God's steadfast and abundant love. One wonders, though, why it is that God seems to be the court of last resort rather than the first and immediate choice of the faithful. Perhaps it is that choice that calls us to prayer, that option that pulls us into community, and that possibility that launches us into ministry.

Could it be that the process of choosing God first in our lives is the one to which the church is called? Could it be that in this psalm can be discovered a focal point and challenge to each and every person? What would this world look like if faithful people chose God and God's way first? What would our congregations look like if prayer and surrender to the Holy were the first items on the agenda?

Psalm 8

"What are human beings that you are mindful of them, mortals that you care for them...?"

Verse 4 of this psalm traverses centuries of theological questing in a single phrase. Its simple, stark question strips away the layered tradition and addled pretense and goes right to the core of a fundamental human struggle.

It goes something like this. If, God *is* God — if this God is the creator; the one — if this God created everything including worlds and things we have yet to imagine, then what are we? The existential question looms larger than a Samuel Becket play. Indeed, as the psalmist puts it, why should God be mindful ... of us at all? And truly, the question has merit. The sheer magnitude of the concept of a creator God sets the writer back on heels of humility and conjures up intermingling scenes of confusion and wonderment.

But in these days of robotics and nano-technology things seem somehow different. As we step into the uncharted territory of interplanetary travel, cloning, and other strange scientific adventures, we no longer see ourselves in the same light as this writer saw (him)self. Today, when global communication comes with the click of a mouse, when world economies are intertwined, and the very ground upon which we stand is changing, the truth is that humanity is not so easily awed as once it was. As we watch creation falter in the face of human activity, the thought occurs to some that perhaps God isn't so great after all.

And herein lies the crux of the issue for people of faith in this so-called post-modern day. Perhaps it can best be voiced, not by a statement, but by a question — this question: What becomes of people who lose their sense of awe? In this psalm, that sense of amazement and astonishment at the width and breadth of the reality of God is palpable. It brings on a powerful sense of thankfulness and gratitude as the author lets a slow breath escape in simple, powerful language.

Without awe, without a sense of wonder at something or someone much larger than ourselves, we run the serious risk of trying to play God. Without awe, arrogance moves in and makes itself comfortable. Without awe, ice caps melt. Without awe, genocide slips by unnoticed — unattended. Simply put, a people without awe are dangerous, and we have become that people.

One can't help but wonder what it might take to recapture a sense of awe; to read this psalm with an open and vulnerable heart. It's certainly worth a try. Read it. One more time with a contrite and broken heart (Psalm 51:17). Maybe, just maybe, we might reclaim the childlike sense of wonder and joy to which Jesus called his followers (Matthew 18:3), then and now.

Psalm 8

This psalm always causes a little consternation. It is one of those passages that seldom finds its way into a sermon. Oh, it gets quoted now and again, but exploring this exposé of the human condition is always a tough thing to do from the pulpit. No good word for the week here. No sage advice or witty metaphor to ease life's struggles. The words here describe an existential truth that rides with each person throughout his or her lifetime, and it is not an easy truth to embrace.

Human beings are somehow "a little lower than God," and simultaneously in charge of business on the planet earth. Above the "creatures," and below God. It's a no-win situation. No matter how hard we may try, we are not possessed of the simple creatureliness that comes, well, with all God's creatures except us! And on the other side of the equation we are not, no matter how hard we may try, even close to being God. Yet here we sit, sentient beings caught in the cosmic in-between.

It is disconcerting.

However, this psalm seeks a way out of this existential mire. This psalm turns our cosmic isolation into a blessing. Is that reasonable? Is that even possible? "What are human beings that you are even mindful of them? Yet you have made them a little lower than God, and crowned them with glory and honor. You have given them dominion over the works of your hands...." Yes. This much is obvious. What are human beings that God should pay attention? A cursory glance will show a rebellious, quarrelsome, and violent species, bent on their own destruction. Yet, they are crowned with God's glory; given a responsible job and a position of honor.

Sometimes a pastor will invite a person in the congregation to do some work that he or she knows she is not presently capable of achieving. The agenda has to do with the person rising to the level of expectation. It has to do with pulling excellence from the shadows of someone's soul.

Could it be that this is the case with humanity? Could it be that we are indeed capable of the job before us as stewards of God's creation? Could it be that God has called us to a job that demands more of us than perhaps we think we can do? Could it be that our existential location is a blessing from God; a challenge from the holy calling us forward?

In a word, "Yes." This could be the case. Indeed, it may well be our reality. So praise God for the challenge and the calling. Praise God for expecting great things of us.

Psalm 8

Knowing one's place in the world is an important thing. Indeed, some would say that it is an essential ingredient in being a full, even sane individual. Without a place in which we belong, we are footloose, adrift, and without connection. Without a niche to call our own we become vagabonds of the spirit, always on the move, always looking for a place to land.

Human history could be described as the never-ending search for just such a place. It is an existential conundrum that finds form in this psalm as the writer ponders what it means to be "a little lower than God...." It is a statement that seems a bit arrogant, but upon examination, strikes home. After all, we have been given "dominion" over the works of God's hands. The sheep, ox, beasts of the fields; the birds and the fish of the sea; all of it is in our hands.

It is a frightful thought, for the truth is that human beings have made a complete mess of things. From the looming catastrophe of global warming to the stripping of the seas of life, our "dominion" has not worked out so well. From growing rates of extinction of a host of creatures to the mowing down of rain forests, one has to wonder if God might have made a slight error in judgment here.

Could it be that humans have only heard part of the reading of this psalm? Could it be that we have embraced the dominion part, but missed out somehow on the part where we are to be in awe of the works of God's hands?

Sure. Humans got the bigger brains, the opposable thumb, and an insatiable drive to expand and control. But did we get the part where we're supposed to love God's creation? Have we taken in the magnitude and glory of this remarkable planet? Or is that mountain in the distance just a hill to be removed so we can get at the coal?

Perhaps the time has come for a holistic embrace of what it means to be stewards of God's creation. Maybe now is a time our species might take stock of the world in which we find ourselves and claim some of that oft discussed "personal responsibility" for the shape in which we have left God's world. Could it be that, like the Holy Trinity, expressed in Creation, Word, and Spirit, our understanding of dominion needs also to be expressed in a threefold fashion?

What if dominion were just one part of a trinity of stewardship? What if there were two other components consisting of compassion and humility? Such an expression of our place in the world might bring a new balance. A holy blend of dominion, compassion, and humility could well be a new expression for how we humans could begin again — as ones who know their place as stewards and caretakers of one of God's incredible gifts — creation itself.

Psalm 9:9-20

There is a well-worn adage that all preachers must endure hearing. It has to do with avoiding politics in the pulpit. It comes from all corners of the faith community and serves to drive the pastor into a somnambulant set of choices when it comes to offering God's word to the people on the sabbath day. Whatever you do, we are told, keep politics out of it.

In all candor, there is truth to this adage. We are not, if we are faithful to our calling, to bring our own political perspectives with us into the pulpit. If we are Republicans or Democrats or Green, or whatever, it matters not. It is a mistake bordering on idolatry to take our ideological preconceptions and try to stretch the holy scripture over them like it is so much plastic wrap. We have seen far too much of this in our country, and it needs to stop.

However, with this said, we do need to authentically reclaim our calling to preach the holy scriptures. If we live into the word, and preach from its heart, then we are simply being faithful. If faithfulness has political consequences, if faithful preaching of the word has implications for how we live our lives out as a people or a nation, then so be it.

This psalm appears to be one of those portions of scripture that, if preached authentically, might have such implications. The writer of this piece did not claim membership in a political party. The pen that scratched out these words didn't do so because of party loyalty. It seems that the stronghold of the oppressed is God. Where else, after all, can they turn? It is the governments of the world that cause the oppression, and they are sinking, we are told, into the pits that they themselves have dug.

If one reads on, the going can get tough. How does this psalm address us as a people of faith? How does it speak to us as citizens of a nation for which we pay the bills and step — or not — into the voting booth? How does our overarching biblical tradition address this? What exactly is our responsibility to the oppressed and the needy? This question comes, not to partisans, but to a people of faith. These questions don't emerge from a political campaign or an ideological think tank. They emerge from our traditions and our scripture, from our faith and our prayers.

Let the answers come, then, from these sources. As we respond in faith, to our faith, let us not worry about the politics. Let us be concerned, instead, with preaching the word of God faithfully and truthfully as best we have the light. Let the politics of "this world" (1 Corinthians 3:19) stake out its ground and make its claims. But let us root our lives, our hearts, and our actions in God's word and God's word alone.

Psalm 13

Certainty is rarely to be trusted. When it comes to human community, to politics, to cooking, and yes, to religion, certainty is best kept at a distance. A healthy respect for ambiguity is often helpful in these and other areas of life.

In human community it's best to lean into flexibility, making allowances, offering forgiveness, and creating space for people to grow and change.

In politics, certainty is often the enemy of truth and justice. A mind made up and unchangeable is not the mind of a good leader. It is, rather, the closed and concretized nature of an ideologue. Situations and people change. Leaders should reflect that.

In cooking, improvisation breeds invention, and invention results in wonderful gourmet delights. Recipes were not meant to be followed like some map to a destination. No, recipes were meant to be accompanied by loving creativity and experimentation. How else would the hundreds if not thousands of new cookbooks published each year be possible?

And religion? Certainty in this arena can be lethal, especially if that certainty is foisted off on others. It's all right to be certain about one's own beliefs and faith. It's all right, as this psalm clearly illustrates, to place your complete trust in the God of Israel. But if we are unable to allow for that same certainty in others who may see the holy in a different light, trouble is likely to emerge.

Personally, this writer likes certainty. It makes things easy. The clarity it gives provides purpose and direction. This is all good and wonderful. Yet it can go horribly wrong if that clarity and purpose drives over the clarity and purpose of someone else, knocking it flat in the process.

So let us sing with this psalmist! Let us join in our shared trust in God's steadfast love. And as we do this, let us leave room for grace, for flexibility, and for just a little ambiguity in our lives and in our faith.

Psalm 14

The concept of atheism is curious. In modern usage, the word refers to someone who doesn't "believe" in God. Most people have bumped into atheists. They come in all shapes and sizes with all manner of reasons for disbelief. Experience suggests, however, that it's not so much God that people reject, but the people and the institutions who claim to represent God.

The word "atheist," however, means literally that someone is without God. The implication is that whether God exists or not, the atheist chooses to do without. And, as our psalmist suggests, here is a fool indeed.

It is not so much that people who believe differently are fools. Nor is it the case that such people are corrupt and prone to abominable deeds. But there is a point to be made here. That point is that many who dismiss God aren't saying that God doesn't exist. They just want the job themselves. In a culture brainwashed to believe in the supremacy of the individual and brought up to think that freedom is the license to do anything we want, this sense that there is nothing bigger, larger, or more powerful than ourselves is ominous.

Consider the case of certain nations who see themselves as all powerful. Since there is no belief in anything more powerful, corruption does indeed ensue as no-bid contracts are handed to buddies and friends, and once unthinkable deeds like torture become the order of the day.

Here it is in a nutshell. Those who do not acknowledge a power beyond themselves are not merely fools. They are dangerous.

In his paraphrase of Psalm 14, Eugene Peterson puts it wonderfully. "God sticks his head out of heaven. He looks around. He's looking for someone not stupid — one man, even, God-expectant, just one God-ready woman. He comes up empty. A string of zeros. Useless, unshepherded sheep, taking turns pretending to be the shepherd."

In our narcissistic reality, it is all about us, isn't it?

Addressing a concern in a recent meeting, a parishioner actually said, "I'll begin with how I feel, because if it feels good to me it must feel good for everyone else." This person was completely serious! If he/she felt fine then of course it must be okay for every-one. What folly! What delusion! And yet, it is the air we breathe. Whether it is a nation blinded by power or an individual drunk on the selfish illusions of culture, we do take turns pretending to be the Shepherd.

And while we dance to this frightening rhythm, God is neither fooled nor pleased. It turns out that God not only exists, God is paying attention. Our arrogance does do damage. Our delusions of power do lead us into corruption and injustice, and we are held accountable.

Psalm 14

It's interesting how words and meanings evolve over time. The word "atheist," means literally, one who is without God. Its root meaning doesn't have much at all to do with believing or not be-lieving. It simply means that a particular person is "without" God. For some years after leaving home as a young man, I deserted church and all its trappings in favor of the university intellectual scene. Personally, I just needed to get away from it. It didn't occur to me that I was without God at the time. But, perhaps, I was.

What does it mean to be without God? Is it a case of rebellion, as it was in my post-adolescent college days? Is it a separation from God? Some might describe that as sin, but that's another topic. So much of what we believe suggests that it's impossible to be without God — that it's difficult to imagine such a state. Unless, that is, we outright reject God.

Perhaps this is the situation that the psalm here tries to ad-dress, labeling as a fool that one who claims there is no God. Some pastors have seen this in people who have suffered horrible trag-edies or traumas. A child is dead for no reason. God takes the rap, of course, and the grieving parent walks away from it all. It is, at least, understandable. What other reasons might there be for re-jecting God? Over the years, the secular scientific world has tried to shed God as it came closer to understanding the universe. Then, of course, there was the famous "God is dead" business in the 1960s. There are, it seems, manifold reasons for rejecting God.

The powerful truth beyond our psalm, however, is whatever state of theological rejection or denial someone may be engaged in, God doesn't reject them. Like parents weathering a child's flailing about in the midst of a temper tantrum, God's patience is epic as human folly unfolds over the centuries.

When I gingerly returned to faith and church, I found that, though I had taken a bit of a break, God had not abandoned me at all. Our God is not a God of abandonment, but rather a God of accompaniment. Even the fool who shouts that there is no God has a God. And, though it grates against the sense, even those who "devour the people," have a God.

The real trick isn't having a God. That part's easy. The tough call is being faithful to God.

Psalm 16

This psalm is a beautiful utterance of loyalty. More than that, it is a profession of oneness, of unity, of an almost sublime acceptance of God's sovereignty in one's life. The quality shown here is a melding of submission and adoration. In this comes the acceptance of limitations in life.

"The boundary lines have fallen for me in pleasant places." How incredible it is to sense one's limitations and accept them. This is no easy thing. We are weaned on the expectation that we will go beyond our limitations. Bursting boundaries and borders is the accepted means of "getting ahead" for most of us. The ambitious among us chafe at boundaries and resist those who would set them. It brings to mind an advertising campaign for one of the major automakers. The leading phrase that touted the product line was, "No boundaries." Frankly, that is a dangerous assumption. Boundaries are everywhere. We find them even in natural law. If one jumps off a cliff, gravity takes over and you fall. It's a boundary. If we dump tons of polluting gases into the air, global warming will happen. It's a boundary. Human relationships are made stronger with healthy and clear boundaries.

Boundaries, in fact, are a hallmark of human existence, and with God such boundaries exist. God gives us "counsel," and "instruction," and shows us the way to go. Choosing God as our sovereign, as our Lord, means that we no longer go our own way. It means that we have chosen a path. It is for us, "the path of life."

Within these holy property lines the people of God can find security, for at the root of it all is the trust we place in God. We accept the boundaries because we trust. And, because we trust we find security and peace, strength and inner joy.

It is as the psalm suggests. "We have a goodly heritage." It is a heritage of faithfulness, of fealty to the one who created us — the one who came so that we might have life ... and that in incredible abundance.

Yes, this heritage has pleasant boundaries. They are borders that make clear our identity. They are the surveyor's marks that tell us we are on the right path. And they are lines that we choose not to cross because we have chosen to trust in God's counsel and to keep "the Lord ever before us."

Psalm 17:1-7, 15

The world in which we live is awash in a media frenzy of image and hype. The images, claims, and counterclaims come so rapidly that it is virtually impossible for anyone to follow the debate, let alone take a side with any sense of accountability. The truth of what is actually happening around us is tragically lost in this sea of so-called misinformation.

In the midst of it all, each person is called to a continual vigilance in terms of seeking out the truth. No one should merely accept what media accounts declare. Reading more than one newspaper, researching stories, and learning about current events is a primary antidote to the smog of lies that constitutes the media today.

There is one other thing that each person must do as we all attempt to navigate the shoals of contemporary society. Each person must maintain their own integrity, honesty, and accountability for their lives. The psalmist here is clear. We shall be tested by the world. Circumstances will try us. And through it all, God calls us to maintain the highest of standards in our own behavior. Whatever is going on in culture or civilization, each person of faith should be able to say with the psalmist, "If you test me, you will find no wickedness in me."

If each person conducts his or her affairs with robust integrity and impeccable honesty it will be ever more difficult for those in power to propagate lies. If each person insists on lives that are above reproach, then those who do not seek the public good will find it harder to get their way. However, if all we do is talk about honesty and point fingers at others while our own deeds do not match our words, it will not only cause our own downfall, but will impede the cause of righteousness and justice.

As this psalm indicates, it doesn't matter what others do. It is incumbent upon us as people of faith to live lives that are as blameless as possible. That way, when testing comes, we will not be found wanting. That way, when crises occur, we will be shown to be true. It turns out that this is more than a matter of pride or reputation. It exceeds any potential embarrassment on our part. As ones who bear the name of Christ, we do our Lord and our cause great damage if we do not embody the same values we preach. If God's love in Jesus Christ calls for love of neighbor, then we ought to be exemplary in the ways we love our own neighbors. If we receive the call to love our enemy in the teachings of Jesus, then we should devote our every waking hour to understanding and loving the enemies we have in our own lives.

This psalm rings out with clarity about God's steadfast love. In the ringing it calls us to a standard of excellence and wonder so that when the testing comes our God will find that we have "held fast to his path."

Psalm 19

"The law of the Lord is perfect...." In a suspicious and cynical generation like this one, such a claim is automatically suspect. In the first place, protestants with sketchy education have learned from Saint Paul that law is not to be trusted. In the second place, again with sketchy educations, any notion of perfection is not only suspect, it is to be discounted. Perfect law? It would be easier to convince the Navy to put screen doors on submarines as it would be to convince this generation of a perfect law of God.

The struggle, though, is compounded when one hears that this law of God is not only perfect, it serves to revive one's soul and even offers wisdom to the simple.

This is a generation of skeptics. Informed by enlightenment thinking and fueled by the myth of scientific proof, people scoff openly at the notion that a precept of the Lord could both be perfect and good.

Yet, it is true. If we understand the "law" of the creator to be written, not only in our sacred texts but in creation itself we begin to get a glimmer of the truth and depth of this claim. Consider some of the more basic laws. The ancient dietary laws were not there merely to set up kosher kitchens. They were there to protect the health of the community. One didn't eat pork, quite frankly, because under food storage conditions of the day, it was frequently fatal to do so. The Ten Commandments are not mere exercises in following the whims of a capricious deity. They are practical, life-giving processes for the purpose of guiding a community.

It makes sense that we should not steal from one another. Rampant theft leads to chaos and chaos to the destruction of community. One wishes some of the predatory lenders working over the past years had heard of such a law. Neither does it take a world-class sociologist to figure out that killing people doesn't lead to a productive and healthy community. So it is that the "Thou shalt not kill" commandment has power for us, especially today.

Yes, the law of the Lord is indeed perfect. Saint Paul's introduction of grace does not relieve us from the sacred calling to follow God's leading. Indeed, following these laws does lead to health, wholeness, and strength.

Perhaps this generation would do well to trade in its skepticism for a modicum of trust and prayerful reflection.

Psalm 19

Saint Paul gave the Christian church a great legacy, and that gift is the truth we proclaim: that grace overcomes law. Paul's writings are shot through with this concept, making this notion central to us in our tradition. It runs through sermons and texts, permeates church doctrine, and causes us to snicker and sneer at the concept of law. Even when our institutions reach pharisaical heights that would have made Jesus flinch, we mouth the verbage of grace over law.

Let's be candid here. Law has gotten a less than deserved, bad reputation. Especially if it's God's law we're discussing. This psalm pushes the point with clarity. "The law of God is perfect, reviving the soul." While it's true that laws and the blind following of them can be destructive, God's laws, if followed, can actually revive our souls. Take the Ten Commandments as a good example. If we don't steal or kill or commit adultery or covet our neighbor's property, even the most unreasonable among us will admit that life will be better. Even the Levitical code, which draws so much ridicule from contemporary analysis, sought to improve the quality of life.

God's law seeks the welfare of the people and the creation in which they live. If the law in question doesn't do this, then the law itself should be questioned. But given this parameter, God's laws are indeed "more desirable than gold," and "sweeter than honey" (v. 26). Think about it. Deuteronomy 26 makes it clear that God's law involves taking care of the "resident aliens," the "widows and the orphans." Indeed, if we care for those who are most vulnerable among us, are we not ourselves the recipients of healing?

Finally, think for a moment about God's call to keep the sabbath. In our world of eighty-hour work weeks and disappearing vacations, pensions, and benefits, what does it mean to keep sabbath? Where is the rest that literally re-creates us? Do we take it? Are we allowed? Do we suffer because of it? The law requiring us to keep sabbath is about far more than getting yourself into a pew each Sunday. It's about authentic rest. This is indeed a "true and righteous" ordinance.

All this being said, it should be understood that Paul is right. Grace overcomes law, but we should take note that God's laws are not the dictates of some silly autocrat. They have, at their core, our well-being and our salvation as their goal. Indeed, "the precepts of the Lord *are* right."

Psalm 19

What a potent poem is rendered in this psalm. The image of God's glory being shouted in a voiceless language sends the mind to spinning. The whole of creation stretches out to declare the wonders of God. Creation gets it right. From a blazing sunrise in the east, to the Maxfield Parrish blue skies at sunset, creation is indeed articulate. Take the view through a microscope, or through a telescope, and from the tiniest to the largest it is abundantly clear. "Our God," as the praise song goes, "is an awesome God."

This psalm, however, nudges us past creation's wonder and speaks to God's law. A law, which the psalmist tells us, is "perfect." With Pauline exhortations about law notwithstanding, there is something to attend to in this. Consider for a moment the notion of a law that can "revive the soul" (v. 7). What kind of law could do this? The contemporary mind rushes to television courtrooms and outlandish lawyers. The immature mind chafes at the notion of rules that would constrict or limit. But the mind that is attuned to the holy might imagine a soul revived by God's perfect law.

Think for a moment about the Ten Commandments. Imagine a nation that actually paid attention to these laws. Picture a place where no one stole anything. That includes burglars and CEOs. This, in itself, would be world-changing, but let's not stop there. What if everyone decided that killing other people simply wasn't going to happen anymore? What if everyone, soldiers, terrorists, gang members, cops, and robbers; everyone laid down their arms and refused to hurt another human being?

"Yes, yes," the accusation can already be heard. "That's so naive."

But the question needs to be asked. "Is it? Is it truly naive, or have we been so encrusted with cynicism that we can no longer envision a community where God's vision — or God's law — is truly lived?" You see, if only these two commandments were actually followed, souls would indeed be revived. There's no question about it. With no stealing or murder (whether by governments or by individuals), fear would evaporate like a puddle in the noonday sun. Without rampant theft, people would stop worrying about their possessions. Fear would vanish. Creativity would flourish. Generosity would blossom. Revived souls? You bet.

More precious than gold? Sweeter than honey? If a people of faith could but imagine these laws fulfilled, a huge step would be taken. And if that same people, having imagined it, would dare to step into the adventure of living in obedience to these laws, the world could literally be healed.

Psalm 19

Many preachers use the last verse of this psalm as a prayer before launching into Sunday's sermon. "Let the words of my mouth, and the meditation of my heart be acceptable to you, O Lord, my rock and my redeemer." It is a prayer that serves as a kind of gentle reminder to the pastor who is beset by all kinds of temptations as he or she steps into the pulpit each Sunday.

Each pastor who forms a weekly message must resist the temptation to use the pulpit inappropriately. Church fights cannot be waged from the pulpit. Favorite political causes ought not be advanced from the pulpit, and self-indulgent whining should never be heard from a pulpit. The words of the preacher's mouth need to be acceptable to God, and as any pastor can easily observe, this is not always an easy thing to achieve.

The person who stands in a pulpit Sunday after Sunday has been given formidable responsibility. Week after week this person must somehow open up God's word to a congregation that waits hungrily for it. It is no easy task, and it is why prayer comes from so many preachers each Sunday. The words need to be "acceptable" to God.

But it is not merely to the pastor that this psalm is addressed, is it? How powerful a thing it would be if each member of each congregation owned this prayer in the way so many pastors utter it. How powerful a witness would emerge if each word and each thought were scrutinized to be sure that they were acceptable in God's sight.

It's true that pastors are frail, and sometimes sermons are questionable as to their probable acceptance before God. But then, aren't we all frail? Would it not be a beautiful covenant to make in a church community that each person would make a special effort to screen the words before they are spoken with the following question. "Is what I'm about to say acceptable to God?" Are the words that are forming in my mind designed to lift up and heal? Are they intended to nurture and bring life?

If such a covenant were made, the immediate result would be that every one would probably speak a lot less than they do now. Worse things could happen in a world so overfilled with empty words.

So what of it? Might a covenant be offered this Sunday? Might all the faithful commit to making the words of our mouths and the meditations in our hearts acceptable before God? It's at least worth a try.

Psalm 20

Everyone wants a protector. It is, as young people are fond of saying, a "no brainer." Life is no bowl of cherries and despite our New Testament Jesus and his calls to love and forgivness, we are not fooled. We know that enemies abound. We all know that everyone could use a protector. Whether it's women who suffer and die from the scourge of domestic violence or homeless people set upon by amoral attackers, a protector is needed. Whether it is workers stripped of their pensions by corporations recording record profits or students no longer able to pay for their education, a protector is needed. Whether it is a youngster in the grip of sexual abuse or the angry, unjust accusations of coworkers or community members, a protector is needed.

Around this troubled globe there are countless scenarios where we can say that a protector is needed. Indeed, the list is so long that the heart grows numb in the reading. Yet, the truth is clear. A protector is needed.

The psalm describes this protector with words that warm our spirits. So powerful is this protector that even the utterance of God's name is protection (v. 1). This protector will fulfill our desires and see our plans come to fruition. This protector will provide us with the victory. This protector is the real deal. Incredibly, this protector is so powerful that we are to abandon our weapons and defenses and place our total trust in him (v. 7). What's that? Come again?

Ah. There's the rub. We want the protection. Who doesn't? But letting go of our own weapons? Abandoning our own right to protect ourselves? That's a bit of a different story. Only a fool surrenders his or her weapons and defenses. For too many of us, the MGM voice of Moses echoes in our souls. They will have to pry our weapons from our "cold, dead hands."

It seems that we would have it both ways. We want the protection, but find it hard to trust the protector. We want the benefits of the relationship, but none of the costs.

This psalm finds us in an all too familiar place. Trusting, really trusting in God just isn't our strong suit, is it? How does that old World War I song go? "Praise The Lord And Pass The Ammunition"? That really isn't what God has in mind for us, is it?

So let us live into the questions. How can we take that giant step of faith? How can we cease to depend upon our puny defenses and trust wholly in God? What will it take for us to release all the baggage we carry and to throw our hearts and souls upon the mercy and wonder of God?

Tough questions. Tougher answers. But in community, in commitment, in forging ahead in faith, they just might be found.

Psalm 22

The opening words of this psalm are the same ones uttered by Jesus as he hung near death on the cross. They are etched across the collective memory of millions who trace his footsteps to Golgotha. Who could blame him for such an outburst? He had been betrayed, arrested, and handed over to the authorities to be tortured. We can be sure that with these folk there was no mincing debates about water boarding. This guy was tortured. No question about it. On top of that he had to carry the instrument of his death on his own back while the fickle crowds jeered and cheered. It's no wonder that he felt "forsaken."

Yet somehow even as these words escaped his lips one wonders if he had the rest of the psalm in mind. Forsaken? Sure. But there's more to it, isn't there? In spite of the spectacular collapse of his ministry there is the flinty and unquenchable faith that will not surrender, even to the agonies of an unspeakable death.

"All the ends of the earth shall remember ... and turn to the Lord...." Left, it seems, by pretty much everyone, the enormity of what is taking place at this moment has to be rooted in the conviction that "dominion belongs to the Lord," and in the foreknowledge that even those who "sleep in the earth" "shall live for him."

For those who live through their own crucifixions in this life, such foreknowledge can offer incredible hope. In the excruciating process of divorce, it can help to know that somewhere in the months or years to come, healing and new life will be available. In the searing grief of loss when a spouse or parent dies, it is good to know that there will be a day when pain subsides. And in those times when it seems like everyone has abandoned us and there are enemies all around, there can be comfort in the truth that our Savior and our Lord has walked this way himself and bids us follow on to a brighter day.

New life is, after all, the promise. So it would indeed seem that even as these words escaped Jesus' lips, he had the rest of this psalm in mind.

Psalm 22

The opening words of this psalm are etched in the minds of millions of people. They are so familiar that even non-Christians who lack any substantive grip on the faith will nod in recognition when they hear them.

"My God, my God, why have you forsaken me?" Of course, the words stay in memory because they are uttered at a high point in the Holy Week drama. The sacrifice is made, the step is taken, but more than the drama is the fact of our universal ability to identify with the words.

After all, nearly anyone hearing this story can identify with a sense that God has abandoned them. As humans endure suffering across the spectrum of existence, this experience echoes in the heart. After a crushing loss, in the wake of a devastating illness, in the waves of grief after a divorce, or in the maw of grinding poverty, it is easy to feel that the holy one, the one who could wiggle a finger and change it all, has simply packed up and left town. Indeed, even as the computer keys clack out these words, Christians from across the globe continue to wrestle with the question of how a loving God can allow suffering.

But the truth is that God doesn't *allow* suffering at all. It is, perhaps, our idolatrous insistence on imagining God as one of us that allows us to fall into the foibles of such a discussion. The reasoning goes like this. As a parent, who would allow a child to suffer the vagaries of cancer or sexual abuse? Of course, no loving parent would tolerate that. Therefore our Daddy God, who could wave a wand and stop it all, must be cruel. But God isn't like us. Scripture reminds us that God is God: far more awesome and huge than we can comprehend.

So it is that we abandon the finger wagging at God and come to this beautiful truth. It is in the depths of it all that God is most present. Whether it is on the cross or in a hospital bed, in a war zone or a dirty back alley, God accompanies us in our suffering and walks through every moment of our agony with us.

On this day of crucifixion it isn't a God of cruelty we see, but a God of accompaniment; a God who goes through it all as one with us.

Psalm 22:1-15

In each person's life, there comes a moment of defeat and desperation. It is a part of the cycle of our humanness that brings us ultimately to such a time. Sometimes, of course, suffering is self-inflicted. Unwise choices, arrogance, and ignorance certainly add to our seasons of desolation. At other times, travail is brought on by circumstances beyond our control. No matter where the cause is found, that gut-wrenching moment when it feels as though even God has abandoned us is strangely universal.

It is not productive to compare peoples' pain and oppression. However, there is some comfort to be had in the words of this psalm because as we read through these verses we find ourselves on familiar terrain. We have traveled this road ourselves, and it appears that someone has gone before us. It is what one preacher called the "desperation location." Many things can take us to this place. The searing grief of loss through death or a shattered relationship are experiences we all share. We can be transported by conflict, poverty, illness, and of course, war. Many arrive at this point as we stare into the jaws of our own death. It is not for nothing that Jesus chooses this psalm to quote as he hovers in agony, moments from his own death.

Still, though, from the depths of our depravity and suffering, we reach to God for deliverance. Whether it is our psalmist pleading to a God who seems oddly absent, or Jesus gasping what everyone believes is his last breath, we reach for God. It is in the reaching that we find both deliverance and clarity. Indeed, it may be that without reaching we will find neither.

Through the smog of our own confusion-limited vision one thing becomes clear. It is God who rescues. We may depend upon many other things and people for our security and our salvation, but it is God who delivers. Sure. We all want our Social Security checks when we get old, though this may be less available than we hoped. We all like to depend upon some semblance of civil order and freedom, though the times can erode these as well. We all like to feel safe from that which we fear, though fear can be manipulated with frightening ease. All of this is part of our daily reality, and it is a good thing to acknowledge. Still, it is God who saves. None of our machinations or preparations, in the end, will help. When we awaken to find ourselves in that "desperation location," let us "commit our cause to the Lord, and let him deliver...."

Psalm 22:23-31

Take a look around and conduct an informal survey. Who is it that we lift up in our culture? What kind of people garner praise and adoration? Who is it that causes us to pause and nod in affirmation? The answers come quickly, don't they? In our culture, those who gain adoration are celebrities. They are famous for little else than the fame that mass media brings them. Adoration comes to pop singers, athletes, and movie stars. It comes to those who are successful in business. Think of the tycoons who populate the television screen in what is frighteningly labeled as "Reality TV." It's safe to say that our standards have been lowered.

Yet, the psalm before us offers some hope. It directs adoration, obviously, to God. This is, after all, a psalm! But in the cultural smog of celebrity and five-minute fame, it might be useful to note why it is that God is adored here.

God's looks don't come into play. Sex appeal isn't much of a factor, either. God doesn't play football or record insipid love songs, and he doesn't gain fame for his wealth. What is it about God that draws the song of adoration from our lips?

It is excellence.

God towers, here, not as a pop icon, but as a standard to which we aspire. God does not, like so many of us, ignore the afflictions of the poor and the afflicted, but stops, turns, and is attentive to their cry (v. 24). God even listens to us. The generations are drawn to God because of the many good things God does. The hungry are fed and satisfied (v. 26), and the writer of this psalm calls the people to sing a song of praise.

So it is that adoration should be given, not to a flash in the pan, but to those who serve the needs of others. God is wonderful because God listens and responds. God is adored because God responds to the needs of the people. Stop a moment. Take another quick survey. Who is it that you know who stops and listens? Who is it that serves the needs of others? Who is it that concerns him or herself with the needs of the poor and the afflicted?

For this is greatness. This is excellence. This is the example of a God who indeed deserves our praise and adoration. This is the voice of a God who calls us to respond in turn and share such wonder with a world that needs it so desperately.

Psalm 22:25-31

A cursory read through of these verses could leave us with the impression that everyone must turn to God ... or else. While Christians are comfortable claiming God's sovereignty in our lives and sharing that good news, is it right to insist that everyone else accept that sovereignty? In a pluralistic world like ours this is a tricky question. Should all the families of the nations bow down before our God? And this dominion that we so freely accept: Do we have the right to force it upon others?

As a Christian writer who accepts the lordship of Christ in his life and has given that life to serving Christ, I have to say that I am most comfortable offering Christ to anyone. It's hard to keep such good news to oneself. However, I balk at forcing it onto someone who says, "No." Moreover, I hesitate to challenge a person of faith, whose faith is not exactly like mine.

If God does have total dominion, which we clearly believe, doesn't it seem likely that God also approves of different ways of worshiping "him"? Otherwise, why would such diversity in faith traditions exist? What if the *authentic* world religions are like languages spoken by different cultures to a God who is far beyond our ability to grasp? This writer speaks the United Methodist dialect of Christianity. Even within Christendom, what other languages exist? From Mennonites to Orthodox, to Quakers and Episcopalians, and back again, we all speak to the same God, don't we? Is it too far a stretch, then, to assume the Muslims, Jews, Buddhists, and others also reach to God in an authentic voice?

What are we to do? If we make space for other expressions of faith, what does this say about our claims? If we acknowledge the legitimacy of other faith traditions, doesn't this somehow de-legitimize our own?

The answer to that question would be, "No." Perhaps the best thing Christians can do is to adopt a New Testament paradigm of allowing God to be the one who judges others (Matthew 7:1; Luke 6:37; John 8:15; Romans 2:1; James 4:12). Perhaps we would be better off if we simply lived out our faith, offering it humbly to others while respecting those who differ and are different. It even might be that our faith could deepen as we interact with others who connect with God differently than we do.

In the meantime, let us look to our own faithfulness, to our integrity in Christ, and leave the judging to God.

Psalm 23

This psalm sits with incredible familiarity on the couch next to us. Like an old friend caught up in the warming embers of faded and familiar stories, the words slide easily over the tongue as we recite these words.

This, to a large degree becomes a problem as we seek to understand this psalm. Most people who read scripture tend to read it as though it were a monologue from the mouth of God. A straight narrative offered like a lecture given to yawning rows of university students. But this isn't the case.

Holy scripture is a conversation. Sometimes it's a dialogue, sometimes it's as though a room full of voices were shouting out in praise and power, but it should never be approached as a monologue.

This is true of Psalm 23 as well.

From the very beginning there is a conversation with an unheard voice. The Lord is my shepherd. The emphasis here needs to be on the word "Lord." In other words, there are choices to be made here. Other shepherds are available. But the writer has made a choice, and it's not king or ruler of the moment. It's not the latest self-help guru or real estate tycoon. It is the Lord!

The tone is oppositional. He (and no one else) makes me to lie down. He (and no one else) leads me beside still waters. He (and no one else) restores my soul. It would be a good thing if this entire psalm could be read with this kind of choice in mind. It is at once a joyful and defiant tone. The trust described here is so total that it banishes fear, even in the face of one's enemies. The words to the old hymn come to mind. "Here I plant my Ebenezer!"

Such a reading flies in the face of the old comfortable view of this piece. Such shifts, however, are often helpful. As the church lumbers toward a new awakening, one has to wonder if there are other scriptures once thought comforting that might now be stirring or even provocative?

Indeed the whole question of comfort comes up as we claim a fresh perspective. Is Christian faith designed for our comfort? Is our church supposed to meet our felt needs? Or is all this really about making a choice of who it is we will follow?

Psalm 23

My daughter hates going down into our basement. Adolescent fears, real and imagined, coalesce within her, making it impossible to go down there with a load of laundry unless our family dog, Charlie, is with her. Charlie makes it okay. He wags his tail and follows her faithfully downstairs and she does the chores required and returns happily to the upstairs world, as long as she is accompanied by Charlie.

Make no mistake, there is no attempt here to equate God with a trained puppy. There is, however, one significant similarity that this psalm underscores. Like Charlie, the faithful family dog, the Lord our God is a God of accompaniment. This is a God who comes with us. The metaphor of the shepherd is more than apt. Always present, guiding, protecting, accompanying the flock, the Lord is simply there. God walks us to green pastures for rest and restoration. God guides us on the pathways of justice and hope.

Even in the worst of times, God is present. This constant, ever-present Spirit gives comfort and even removes our fear. Why? Simply because we know God is there? Truth be told, we don't know it. But we do trust that it is so, and this is the core of faith. Just like my daughter who trusts that the dog is trotting down the steps behind her as she descends into the basement, we know that God walks with us, too, even in our darkest hours.

At the end of the day this proves to be enough. In fact, it's abundance. Our cup overflows, even when it is set on a table across from our worst enemy. There is goodness, mercy, gladness, and yes, a palpable sense of wonder as this God is both contemplated and experienced.

What could be better? Our own accomplishment? Our own ability to define ourselves or to control our environment? We all know how that works. No, in all this, as Saint Paul so powerfully writes, "We are more than conquerors" (Romans 8:37). Because there is nothing that can ever separate us from the love of God in Jesus Christ. There is nothing that can separate us from this God who accompanies us. There is nothing that can remove us from the flock of this shepherd who is our Lord.

Psalm 23

Today's psalm is a poem for those who have planted their standard in the ground. It speaks to those who have made the choice and committed themselves to the God of Israel. "The *Lord* is my shepherd," and no other. From a host of idols and wannabe gods this is the *one*. This is the one who causes us to rest, who restores us, who walks with us into harm's way. In this commitment we find remarkable results.

This most familiar of psalms, this poem of comfort and commitment sits easily with those who have made the commitment. It feels good to have a shepherd God who watches over us. But more than simply observing us, this God accompanies us through the darkest valley. This God is so present that we are able to cease being afraid. What wonders emerge from hearts that are unafraid!

This is also a psalm for the weary and burned out ones; for those whose souls need restoration. It is a missive for the workaholic who is subsumed by work and rushes headlong into exhaustion and collapse. As a friend once commented wryly, "God *makes* you lie down in green pastures." The implication, of course, is that if we don't take sabbath, our spirits and our bodies will rebel. We will become emotionally unstable, and our bodies will grow ill. God will, quite literally, make us lie down.

And for those whose spirits have been wrung dry by the vagaries of conflict and strife, there is a God who sets the table of reconciliation and new beginnings. You are anointed with healing and the cup of abundant life overflows. You don't have to go it alone any longer.

41

Indeed, this psalm flies in the face of a culture that trumpets individualism and going it alone. It lays bare the delusion of independence and opens up the beauty and joy of surrendering to a God who is a partner for the journey; a God who lifts us up when we fall; a God who offers goodness and mercy throughout life.

Finally, this psalm is a call to "dwell in the house of the Lord forever." No, it doesn't mean that we move lock, stock, and barrel into the fourth pew on the right. Rather, it is an invitation to live into the rhythms and dance steps of God. It is a bidding to step into a way of being that is free of fear and anxiety, a path where we are wholly dependent upon God. Perhaps another way of rendering that last line is, "I shall live according to God's reality all the days of my life."

Psalm 23

What Sunday school child cannot recite this psalm? It is an iconic piece of sacred literature that spreads far beyond the doors of church or synagogue. It is read at funerals of atheists and recited in rote rhythms at many a public event. Like cliches, however, the psalm has become so widely known for a reason.

These are powerful words of comfort that echo almost universally as they are read. Who can resist a God who leads the faithful to still waters, who restores the soul and accompanies us through the darkest valley?

This psalm is indeed marvelous. Yet there is a more subtle message in this psalm that is seldom discussed or mentioned. That is, the notion that the words offered here are somewhat oppositional. In other words, the psalmist is writing, not only about a God of comfort and accompaniment. This author is writing about choosing to worship this God. "The *Lord* is my shepherd." There are, it turns out, other shepherds who would try to comfort, who would attempt to gather the sheep. But The Lord is *my* shepherd. Each phrase can, and perhaps should be read with this sense of choice in mind. "*He* (and no other) leads me in right paths...." "*Your* rod and *your* staff — they comfort me."

Putting the emphasis on the notion that the writer is making a choice helps as people wrestle with the many shepherds who are jostling for position and loyalty. The choice of the psalmist, though, is clear — as is ours — the *Lord* is our shepherd.

It is this kind of clarity of choice that is needed as the church navigates the shoals of the so-called post-Christian world. Reading this psalm with this sense of choice speaks to an intentionality and a realization of the powers and the principalities that operate in our world.

Such a reading also accepts the responsibility of making the choice. It is a proactive move toward the Holy God of Israel in the context of a world that seems at times to be afflicted with a spiritual version of attention deficit disorder.

So pray Psalm 23 one more time. Only this time do so with the sense that this is not only a psalm of comfort. It is also a psalm of one who has made a choice, who has made a commitment to this God in whom we choose to dwell forever.

Psalm 24

It is an easily embraced equation. If you're good, you go to heaven. If you're bad, you go — well — you know where. It is precisely this notion that the psalmist here appeals to when we hear who it is that gets to "ascend the hill of the Lord." Wouldn't it be wonderful if this were true? The good, the upright, and the just get to be with God. Those who don't lie, cheat, or steal get to "stand in God's holy place," and "receive a blessing" from God. The only problem is that it's not true.

Writings like this bring out the cynic in our twenty-first-century hearts. Were things different when this writer was scratching the words onto parchment? No. Things were not different. And if we pay attention to our story, we know that the psalmist — though well intentioned — is missing some important details. Jacob, in a deal that would be the envy of any oil baron, took Esau's birthright for a bowl of soup. Moses, wanted for murder, led the people across the Sinai. Paul, chief pursuer of the followers of the way, became himself an apostle.

Who is it that gets to go up that hill? It turns out that it's not the good ones. In fact, the good ones sometimes get short shrift. After all, Job was "blameless" (Job 1:1), wasn't he? And let's not forget the holy innocents who died at the point of Herod's sword while Jesus escaped into Egypt.

There's no getting around it. God seeks out the frail, the broken, the fallen, and bids them step up to the plate. God reaches out and seizes the heart of a prostitute or a tax collector and invites them to the table.

So what's the deal? If God is on the lookout for human wreckage, what motivation have we to be upright and good? If a thief can enter paradise at Jesus' side, why are we wasting our time being truthful, just, and honest? Are we to "sin that grace may abound"? (Romans 6:1).

For us, the answer is found in the voice of Jesus who said that those who are well have no need of a physician (Luke 5:31). God seeks out those whose hearts *need* healing. The uplifting of the downtrodden does not excuse us from God's call to be just and true. We do not enter into faith as a business transaction, bartering with God for favors based on good behavior. No, we step into faith and follow, not seeking results nor looking for reward, but in all things discerning and trying our level best to do God's will. God will deal with all the others in God's own way and God's own time. The rest of us will stand where we have always tried to stand — on the "promises of God our Savior."

Psalm 24

In American culture, the concept of property is primary. Owning things has a great deal to do with our self-understanding and our way of life. There are tomes of laws and legal briefs dealing with property concerns. Hundreds of thousands of people sue one another over property issues. Our energies are squandered in a mindless drive to own more and more stuff. There's no question about it. We are a people obsessed with who owns what, who's going to get to own it next, and how much we own.

One supposes that it's an outgrowth of what we like to call capitalism. It would be a simple thing to descend into a judgmental rant about materialism, but a bit more difficult to confront the reality in which North Americans exist. What's wrong with owning property, anyway? Anyone reading this, including the author, owns quite a bit of *stuff*. Cars (usually more than one), houses (sometimes more than one!), electronic gadgetry, toys for young and old; everyone owns *stuff*, don't they? We worked for it! It's our right to purchase and to own, isn't it?

Yes, but a biblical people living in a culture such as this needs to pause occasionally to consider the path we are taking. As people rooted in the Judeo-Christian heritage, do we really believe that *we* get to own property and material goods? Or could it be that we are entrusted with such things by the true owner and expected to act as responsible stewards?

If we are unclear about this, Psalm 24 serves to help clarify things. The psalm opens with these simple words: "The earth is the Lord's." Well, that settles that. The deed to the house doesn't mean much in light of this. The title to the new car seems worthless. It all belongs to God. Moreover, it seems that we, too, belong to the creator.

And, as a people who belong to God, we are confronted with some expectations. The first is that we are to have "clean hands and pure hearts." This is a question well worth investigating. As ones who belong to the "king of glory," are our hands clean? Are our hearts pure? This psalm calls us to clear and careful discernment here. This discernment begins with a prayerful focus on a few questions.

Does our material wealth have a negative impact on others? Are others hungry while our citizens battle obesity? Do we live in large homes while others wander the streets with no place to lay their heads? What effect does our lifestyle have on God's creation? These are difficult questions, to be sure. But as ones called to faithfulness in Christ Jesus, they are worth asking, praying over, and seeking God's will in the answers.

Psalm 25:1-10

Trusting is never easy. Even in the best of relationships, people step into trust slowly. There is wariness — questioning — worry. What happens if trust is betrayed? What if this doesn't work? Sometimes it's like a dance. We step in and out of trust, moving to the rhythms of fear. For many, the routine is achingly familiar. Indeed, it's not easy to trust.

And when it comes to trusting God the process can be the same, only more so. The writer of this psalm is a case in point. "In you I put my trust, O God. Don't let me be put to shame." In other words, I trust you God, but I'm a little nervous. Here there is a dance of fear, as well. The writer of this piece declares (his) trust while reminding God about mercy and love, just in case the deity might forget. "And God? You're not going to remember that time I messed up really bad, are you?"

The nervousness of this writer belies the myth of absolute belief. In spite of the storm of voices claiming unshakable and certain belief, the truth is that many struggle and stumble into faith. Like this psalm, we believe, but we want to be sure that God's not going to let us down. We believe, but will God hold our past against us? "We believe ... help our unbelief" (Mark 9:24).

Finally, though our psalm writer will not go there, it comes down to grace. We waltz in and out of our willingness to trust the Holy, while God remains faithful. We slip and slide on the highway of our fear and insecurity and God loves us still. More than that, God's love for us trumps our frailties and predates our litany of failures and foul-ups. In fact, God's grace takes the initiative and reaches out for us even as we duck and weave in our vain dance of fear.

The message comes to all people, especially those who wrestle with trust. Even if we are fainthearted and inconstant, God stands firm. No matter what the rhythm of our dance, God seeks to cut in, to be our partner. The bottom line is that God is greater than our worry, deeper than our mistrust, and more gracious than our inconstancy.

Comfort, then, can be taken as we struggle toward faith. Others before us have struggled, too. And they, like us, have met with the awesome wonder of God's grace.

Psalm 25:1-10

This first Sunday in Advent is the beginning of a powerful journey. On this day, Christian community steps onto the birthing path together. It is a time of expectancy. It is a time of pregnancy, both in the sense of Mary's gestation, and our own. And, as any woman who has given birth can tell you, pregnancy is a time of anticipation, pain, wonder, deep intensity, fear, and exhilaration. There is no other time like it.

As we follow this pathway to the stable door, we "lift up our souls to God" (v. 1) in surrender to God's will and ways. This surrender, this placing of trust in God is no mean feat. For most people who attempt it, this process of submission becomes a lifelong journey, and not a task we finish up with a six-week course, like Lamaze or some other birthing class offered at the hospital.

Trusting God is, in many ways, like trusting anyone. Trust means risk. Like the dad who entrusts his new car to his teenage son for a date, like lovers falling into relationship, risk is involved. Things can happen. Things do happen. This sense of foreboding is heard and felt in this psalm. Trust is offered, but there is tenuousness in the writer's voice that fills the heart with empathy. We know, with the psalmist, that trusting in God will not necessarily keep us safe. Indeed, sometimes this birthing path will lead directly to suffering's gate and beyond.

New life can be like that. Pregnancies are full of risks. Our birthing path, too, has risks. When Christian community moves with intention toward new life, risks are there. But for Mary and for us, the promise of new life keeps the heart on the path that leads to Bethlehem. Our trust, even if it is at times a nervous trust, is in God, upon whom we wait. While we wait, we ponder with anticipation the floodgates of new life that are about to open in Christ Jesus.

Psalm 26

Integrity is a precious thing indeed. Upon its firm foundation is built a life that counts for something. If we lose our integrity, we lose a great deal indeed. A person of integrity is trusted. A person of integrity can be counted upon. A person of integrity follows through on commitments.

A good self-examination every once in a while is the one that looks at personal integrity. It can be done quite simply with a few earnestly asked and honestly answered questions:

1. Do you tell the truth in as far as you are able?
2. Do you do the things you say you'll do?
3. Do you speak up or take a stand in the face of injustice?
4. Do you act in ways that would find approval in God's eyes?
5. Are you gentle, caring, and compassionate?

There are, of course, a host of other questions that could be asked. But these five give a good beginning.

The trick in all this is to be able to maintain integrity when things go south. As the psalmist appeals to God, reminding (him) of integrity kept, we ourselves are reminded that good behavior is not always rewarded with a pat on the head.

Indeed, our faithfulness may well cost us dearly. Taking a stand for someone or something could cost us a job or a friend. Being clear about love can raise up resistance from all kinds of locations. The graves of the martyrs the world over can attest to this.

Yet, this integrity is a thing worth keeping. In fact, when the smoke clears and all is said and done, integrity may be all we really have. Maintaining integrity, of course, is not merely a personal, private matter. We must maintain integrity in our communities. Primarily, we must maintain integrity in our churches. In what ways does the church have integrity? In what ways does it not? Do we worship a God of forgiveness on Sunday and fail to practice that forgiveness in our community life? Does our church confess its sins on Sunday and then reap the profits from monies invested in businesses that harm and hurt people? What does the integrity of a church look like? Can the church "wash its hands in innocence"?

Like each one of us as individuals, a church with integrity is not promised wealth and prosperity. A church with integrity may well encounter the cross. Yet it is this integrity, if we can maintain it with authenticity, that will save the church. It is faithfulness — nothing more; nothing less — that God desires.

Psalm 27

Little children love to walk on the edge. They can be seen constantly balancing on fences, curbs, and tree branches as they test their sense of balance and seek the boundaries of their existence. And indeed, as this powerful psalm shows us, life is a balancing act. No naive transactional relationship here. No quick cash deal. This writer does not presume that fidelity to God will erase the presence of enemies and hardship. No. The realization that such turmoil is part of life's landscape seems clear and unequivocal.

It is not the hardship that the writer seeks to jettison. It is the fear. And in order to step into life in confidence, one needs trust. So the real balancing act here is not from the heights of an apple tree or on the edge of a busy highway. The balancing act here is between fear and trust.

The first verse asks the question not once, but twice. If God is my salvation, of whom shall I be afraid? It's a rhetorical question, isn't it? Most of us know quite well who it is that we need to be afraid of in our lives. Most of us know quite well that in the muck and mire of our daily existence, there are adversaries who are real and dangerous. It is a tenuous question that attempts to sort out the issue of trust in God. The narrative reasons cautiously, saying, "If God is who [he] says [he] is then I don't need to be afraid. There is a pause, then comes the question, 'Do I?' "

This psalm reflects our own balancing act between trust and fear in terms of our relationship with God. In the midst of our own trials and suffering, we, too, dance back and forth between the pleas that ask God to save us from our enemies and the intrinsic sense that if we really trust God we don't have to fear our enemies. We, too, beg God to help us. We, too, plead with God not to be angry with us for serial infidelities to (him). And we, too, finally realize that if we trust in God, if we "wait on the Lord," we will "see the goodness of the Lord in the land of the living."

Psalm 27:1, 4-9

German playwright, Bertolt Brecht, writes in one of his immortal tunes that "magic fear puts the world at your command." Writing, as he did, in Germany during and after WWII, Brecht knew something of fear. He knew also how fear was used to manipulate people into doing things that they would not normally consider doing at all. The Nazis made effective use of propaganda to make people afraid of the Jews and were thus able to gain their permission — and at times full cooperation — in the extermination of more than eight million human beings.

Fear is a powerful tool, indeed. Advertisers use it to get people to buy things. Governments use it to control populations, and yes, even religion has used it. But the truth is that as a people of faith we are called out of fear and into faith. As this psalm opens it makes clear to us that *the antidote to fear is not armaments, protection, or aggression, but faith.* "The Lord is my light and my salvation, whom shall I fear?"

For most people, a life free of fear is difficult to imagine. If you are a parent, there are a host of fears centered around raising children. Will they get hurt? Will they be taken advantage of? Will they succeed? Will they be happy? Most parents pour their lives into their children out of love, it's true. Yet, it is also true that this love is mixed with fear. Fear stalks us as we walk the streets, navigate through our careers, or even as we watch the evening news.

Yet here, in these powerful ancient words, liberation from the paralysis of fear is offered. Faith, which in most New Testament translations actually is rendered more accurately as "trust," is the thing that can conquer our fear. A wise preacher once said that "Jesus conquered fear before he conquered death." It's not that Jesus, fully human, was unafraid, it was that he chose trust over fear.

This same option is open to people of faith today. As individuals, we can choose to trust in God and God's way of love rather than give in to the vagaries of fear. In our relationships, too, faith in God can conquer our fear and drive us deeper into love and new beginnings. The same call to trust and faith follows us into life in Christian community and even into our lives as citizens.

"If the Lord is the stronghold" of life, what can possibly make us afraid? If the Lord is our light, we will see hope, love, courage — not fear.

Psalm 29

Anyone who has ever worked with other people knows that it's important to give credit where it's due. If a coworker does a good job on a project, he or she should be acknowledged for a job well done. If a supervisor or boss has people working for him or her, it's common knowledge that praise given for work done is not only a good idea, it makes good business sense.

Yes, it's a pretty simple formula, and most people live by it in one form or another. If the child gets a good grade in school, the parents offer praise. The friend does a favor, she gets the voice of thanks. And if someone "goes the extra mile" (Matthew 5:41), we turn up the volume of praise.

This psalm comes with the volume on high! Giving God the praise, the credit, and the glory flow from these words with breathtaking clarity. The greatness and wonder of God is harvested in words that span a dizzying spectrum. From the giddiness of a young calf to gale-force winds that lay whole forests to waste, God's power is present and in charge. From the mystic beauty of ocean's depth to the visceral boom of thunderstorms close at hand, God sits, as the psalmist notes, "on the throne."

Indeed, it's a good thing to give credit where it's due. Not only is it the right and honest thing to do, it's also a source of relief. That's right. God's in charge, not me. Alleluia! If I'm not in charge, then I don't need to be in control. And if I don't need to be in control, then I can release my spirit and my heart for obedience, not to my desires, but to God's!

For these reasons, praying this psalm is a powerful way to center the spirit and orient the heart. Placing God at the center, giving

God the glory and the credit, and then removing ourselves from the drive to control are key components on the path to faithfulness.

And, like our conversion to faith, which ever unfolds in prayer and faithfulness, this is not a prayer said only once. This is a prayer repeated often as we learn ever and always to give ourselves to God's sovereignty in our lives. So it is that we "ascribe" to God the glory and the splendor. So it is that we give ourselves to God in worship, not merely on Sunday mornings, but in each moment of our lives.

Psalm 29

Certain people have unforgettable voices. Among them are some of the great preachers God has sent us in recent years. The late William Sloane Coffin comes to mind, with his voice ringing out from the pulpit at Riverside Church in New York City. Here was a voice of power. His eloquence and clarity led a generation into faith-based work for peace and social justice. Anyone who ever heard him preach remembers his voice.

. Of course, there was the voice of Martin Luther King Jr. The passionate cadence of his preaching led a movement that looms large in history. His spirit, infused with God's, flung his words to millions who responded by joining the good work for racial justice and peace.

There are many voices that have come to us over the years. Preachers, prophets, community leaders, and even a few politicians have stood out as their voices reached out to the multitude. The utterances are clear, recognizable, and filled with power. Remembering the sounds of these voices leads us into a reading of this psalm as we prepare to hear the "voice of the Lord." It is a voice that seizes us through the awesome panoply of nature. The psalmist hears it in the thunder and listens to it as it hovers over the waters in unimaginable creativity and wonder. The voice of the Lord is full of majesty. It can shatter mighty trees and it can cause us to dance for joy.

When was the last time such a voice was heard among us? Has the voice ceased to speak? Or have we forgotten how to listen?

Truth be told, it is difficult enough to listen, even to one another, in the cacophony of the world in which we live. How is it that we can stop what we're doing long enough to listen for the voice of the Lord?

Not an easy call, is it? But there it is.

This psalm grabs us by the collar and calls us to focus upon God. This psalm bids us let go of our projects and our addiction to being in charge and calls the reader to give all the glory to God. In other words, God gets all the credit, not you or me. It is, after all, God who is the focus of our worship. And it is, perhaps within the wonder of such focus, that the voice of God becomes discernible.

How is it, then, that our communities can stop the business of projects and fund-raisers? How is it that the flurry of programs and ministries can be stilled so that a people might focus on hearing the "voice of the Lord"?

It could be, as this psalm indicates, "hovering over the water." It could also be in the wonder of our children or in the joy of authentic community. This voice, this Word, that comes finally to us in the person of Jesus, is something that each person of faith needs to hear.

The trick, it seems, is learning how to listen.

Psalm 29

Riding out a storm can be an amazing experience. As some of our brothers and sisters in the Gulf Coast can attest, it can also be a time of terror. When the skies thunder and the mighty waters surge, cities disappear. When wildfires devastate huge areas of land, consuming villages and towns; when tornadoes swoop down and erase homes and lives, hope can take a beating.

The psalm, of course, attributes such disasters to the "voice of the Lord." In our circumstances, however, such finger pointing might be better aimed at human negligence. The care of levies and dams, the development of fire-prone areas, and the suppression of natural forest fires are instances that might bear examination before we level an accusatory finger at the almighty.

No matter who we blame, it seems that the storms do come. And with them, the testing of our hope and faith. Hurricanes, forest fires, tornadoes, hunger, injustice, and war all wash over us in waves of devastation, leaving the people crying out for the "blessing of peace" (v. 11b).

Even describing such things leaves the soul weary. It's hard to hope when one is tired. It's hard to reach for a blessing when weariness has robbed us of the strength even to lift up our arms.

Here is where the shallow faith of transaction meets its doom. The brittle barters of belief in exchange for protection are here exposed for the fraud that they are. Our faith, it turns out, is deeper than a curbside trade. Our faith requires more than minimum monthly payments. Our faith, it turns out, is not for the faint of heart.

It is at times like these, when hearts are battered and our spirits worn, that God's voice truly offers strength. It is in moments such as these, that hope's death finds resurrection in the voice of the holy, and it is in the wreckage of our dreams that hope is born again.

Riding out a storm is never easy. We may find ourselves as refugees in foreign lands or prostrate on ravaged ground where once our lives were lived. We may awaken to unimaginable devastation or wander about in numbness and confusion. Whatever the damage, or wherever we may find ourselves, we know one thing is certain: The voice of the holy will always seek us. The voice of the holy can always revive us. The voice of the holy will give us peace.

Psalm 30

One hears a lot these days about habits, good and bad. Most everyone has given up smoking. We are urged to lose the habit of snacking too much. Lord knows that not enough of us have the good habit of regular exercise. No matter what the current hype may tell us, there's no doubt that we need to develop some good habits. Most pastors would love to see people in the habit of tithing. Imagine a whole nation with the habit of exhibiting good manners? No more road rage; no more cussing in public.

Another good habit might be for us to give credit where it's due. How often do good people step up to the plate to offer their hard work and service and receive little or no acknowledgment? Of course, no one is supposed to offer such help with a goal of being thanked, but still, it doesn't hurt. In fact, most people will admit that it helps. This psalm endeavors to give credit where it's due. The call for help went out, and it was heard, and it's time to say, "Thank you!"

How often do we look back at our lives and see God's hand in the mix? When times get tough, we may cry out to God, but when we come out the other side, do we turn back to see how God was involved as we made our way through? Indeed, the temptation is to take credit for ourselves. "See how I managed this?" "Look at me! I toughed it out!" And yet, this is the God who does intervene. This is the one who lifts us from the pits of Sheol, who has turned our mourning into dancing. Can we not stop and give a little credit where it's due?

After all, let's consider the track record here. This is a God who sticks by us; a God who — quite frankly — has put up with a great deal. In the context of our lives, an argument or angry exchange often strangles a relationship. A mistake or wrongdoing finds little grace or forgiveness in our world. After the quarrel there is ... distance, but not so with God! Anger may come, but God's love lasts longer! Even on Sinai in the shadow of a golden calf, Moses was able to turn God's anger away (Exodus 32:11 cf).

How much better would our lives be if we could allow our anger to pass? How much stronger would our relationships be if we knew that the love we held was stronger than the disagreements that will most certainly arise. How much more powerful would our churches be if the love we shared was stronger than the bumps in the road that are sure to come? This God can teach us a lot.

And a good student, of course, gives credit to the teacher.

"O Lord, my God, I will give thanks to you forever!"

Psalm 30

What is the difference between happiness and joy? It seems that many of us spend a great deal of time pursuing happiness. Lots of things make us happy. A new convertible, a nice home, a new MP3 player; all these things do make us happy. In fact, the constitution of our nation guarantees us the right to "pursue" our happiness. This is not a bad thing.

But what of joy? This psalm lifts up a God who has "turned my mourning into dancing," who has "taken off my sackcloth and clothed me with joy." On the surface, one might argue that there is little difference between happiness and joy. Maybe joy is a bit more intense. Perhaps happiness is a touch more giddy. Yet, there is something quite different between the two.

Could it be that happiness is more fleeting, while joy is deeper and more permanent? Could it be that happiness is a serial emotion that leaps like a frog from one lily pad to another? Certainly these thoughts are worth considering.

Joy, though, is a soul thing. It is wrapped up and bound by the chords that tie us to our creator God. In fact, God created human beings so that they might experience joy. Joy is the vibration that comes when the air of God's Spirit vibrates the instrument of our being and God and human resonate together. This is why music and joy are so closely connected. It's why music is thought of as sacred. Joy is the music made by the intersection of human and divine. It is the dance of sacred partnership.

Happiness can be controlled and regulated. Time at the gym makes some folks happy, but there is only so much time. Joy, however, is hard to control. When our spirits intersect with God's, there is no telling where things will end up, no predicting what wonders might take place. When joy is released, healing and hope flourish. When joy is unfurled like a flag of wonder, the promise of love is laid out before us.

Happiness is fine. Happiness is okay. But in this psalm, we are called to embrace the dance of joy as we learn a new step with our creator and redeemer, the Lord who is our salvation.

Psalm 30

Sometimes it seems like God has taken a powder. No matter how theologically astute or disciplined in spiritual practices one might be, it seems that everyone comes to a moment where it feels like God is somewhere else. In a firefight in Baghdad or an AIDS clinic in South Africa it would be possible to wonder, wouldn't it? As genocide stamps out a people in Darfur and grinding poverty consumes millions, it is tempting to wonder if God is hiding his face (v. 7). But this is the big picture. Such feelings emerge, also, in times of more personal struggle. Loss of a loved one, loss of work, illness, or privation can lead a person quickly from words of praise to sobs of confusion.

What's going on here, anyway? What's the point of this suffering, whether it be the big picture, or one's own living room, what good is it if the world descends into the pit? Will the dust offer praise? Will it spread the word about God's greatness? What good does all this suffering do, anyway?

Good questions, to be sure. Through twenty-first-century eyes, the turn around in this psalm can't help but raise an eyebrow or two. God rises up and comes to the rescue. God, in the scribblings of Psalm 30 comes through like the Lone Ranger in the end, and all is restored. Though weeping "lingers through the night, joy comes in the morning." The time for mourning ends as the sackcloth is taken away and "mourning turns into dancing."

Yes — healing can and does come. Grief slowly gives way to hope, and ancient wounds gradually turn to scars. Wars, though seemingly endless throughout our history, do come to an end. And somewhere, through the veil of tears the soft music of new life can be heard.

This is the music of hope. It is the rhythm and the dance of hope. And, it turns out, it's hope that finally rips off the sackcloth. Hope that holds the cloak of joy for us to try on for size. In the end, through the tumult and tremors, through death and unspeakable suffering, it is hope that taps its foot and bids us sing once again. It is hope that strums a chord and leads us in the song.

Psalm 31:1-5, 15-16

In a bookshelf in my living room sits a testimony to change. On the bottom shelf is a row of 45 rpm records. Among them are greats by Gene Pitney, the Beach Boys, and the Beatles. On the next shelf resides several rows of 33 1/3 rpm record albums. Among these are collections by such greats as Bob Dylan, Jimi Hendrix, and a dizzying assortment of one-album wonders. Above that shelf are a few old 8-track tapes. Remember those? The labels have long since peeled away from these and who knows what music is hidden inside? Yet another shelf reveals scores of cassette tapes, many of which are personal mix tapes including favorite tunes recorded to suit certain moods and times of life. Then, of course, come the CDs. They, too, have fallen away as I plug in my MP3 player, which contains a full 100 days' worth of continuous music.

In what feels like a few short years, the change within the music medium has been tectonic. The pace of it is dizzying, and it shows no signs of slowing down any time soon. It seems that much of life is changing at the same rate as the technology we use to listen to music. Everything is changing. Fashions, employment, housing, even the church! All of it is shifting and moving quicker than most can even perceive.

It's in the midst of the storms of change that the words to the old Lutheran hymn emerge. "A mighty fortress is our God, a bulwark never failing!" Taken from this psalm, these words call us to claim that which will not go away. Through the vapors of a fickle culture we cling to the rock which is our God. Above the squabble and bickering of ideology and politics, we climb upon the rock that is our God.

As we look to this solid rock for safety and security, for something solid in the storm, it seems funny that Jesus used this same language to describe Peter (Matthew 16:18). Volatile, uneven, and finally a betrayer, Peter gets to be a rock as well. Herein is a hint of the possibilities that await us.

There is no doubt that God is our rock and our salvation. There is no questioning that this is the refuge to which we cling, but in Christ Jesus there is the possibility of partnership in and with this rock. It is no accident that Jesus called Peter the rock, and for us it is a hint of our own salvation.

If Peter can rise above his failure to be a foundation stone for the church, what might be possible for you and me? How is it that the unmoving, unmovable love of God can move in and transform us so that we too might be foundation stones for the building of the kingdom?

In this time of new life and new hope such questions are worth pondering. Such possibilities are worth embracing.

Psalm 31:9-16

At first, this psalm conjures up the words of an old acquaintance who frequently would call on the phone to say that "I'm not paranoid, they really are out to get me!" It was always offered with tongue-in-cheek. This response, of course, is smarmy in the extreme and offers the benefit of not having to engage the text. But then in the rereading, the protective layers of cynicism fall away and visions begin to emerge.

As the words sink in, images of genocide in Darfur, of rancid hospitals in Bagdad, and rotting homes in New Orleans begin to grow clear. The oft-avoided, always-dreaded suffering of the other comes into focus as knuckles of compassion knock at hardened hearts.

Who has known someone at the end of their rope? Who has sniffed the odor of despair and desperation? And who, sensing that the bucket of options is empty, finally turns and gives it all over to God?

This psalm is a portrait of what one might call a Job profile. It just doesn't seem like it can get much worse, and somehow in the thick of it all one has the odd sense that the cosmic casino is laying odds on the outcome. This is a life washed over with grief and misery; a smashed and broken remnant shrinking from "terror all around."

Yet trust is placed in God because God, it seems, is in charge.

The notion that the "times are in God's hands" is not one exclusive to this setting. Indeed all times are in the hands of God.

Prosperity and abundance, tragedy and despair, joy and sorrow; it's all in the grip of God's sway.

The funny thing is that when we are at the end of our rope, we somehow understand this. This truth is expressed by the old saw that says there are no atheists in foxholes. As the delusion of control is stripped away and lives spiral downward, a turn to one more powerful seems inevitable.

But when the good times roll, things are different. When bellies are full and beds are warm it's easy to live into the delusion that we're in charge of it all, that we are somehow responsible for our good fortune. Grateful hearts somehow dissipate in the face of super abundance.

If only we could ride on waves of consistency and trust in both good times and bad. If only we could look from windows of prosperity to see the pain of others and unlock our hardened hearts.

Psalm 31:9-16

There are times when paranoia is a well-founded emotion. Sometimes people are out to get you. It's an unpleasant truth but a truth, nonetheless. Certain pastors reading this can readily nod in agreement as they recall brushes with angry and often unwell parishioners who pour their life's venom out upon the clergy. Others have felt it when life simply goes wrong. An old friend, going through a series of life struggles, called it his "Job profile."

Times like these occur in most peoples' lives, and they are horrid. It is scant comfort that, in reading this psalm, we find we are not alone. Listed here is everything from being a social outcast to the hatching of evil plots. There is whispering in the air ... "terror all around!" (v. 13).

To contemplate this "Job profile" is to feel a shudder down the spine.

What do we do when we hit bottom like this? What do we do when the platitudes and self-help manuals fall uselessly to the floor, and we are skewered with grief and failure? Some give up. They slip beneath the waters of despair and are seen again only as shells of their former selves. Some fight, and we all know that in fighting there is usually indiscriminate carnage. Some, a precious few, turn to God.

A missionary, who recently returned from a grueling two years working in AIDS ministry in Africa, made this comment upon return: "I now know without one shred of doubt that God loves me completely."

It's an odd, but true, thing. In times like these, many people actually find a deeper connection with God. Perhaps this is because other sources of support and succor are quickly exhausted in times of extended crisis, and we are left with nowhere else to turn. Or maybe it's because it is exactly in times of great testing that God's love and grace are most palpable. Whatever the reason one turns to God, it needs to be said that in the final analysis, it is God, and not despair or fighting, that will see us through our life crises.

Trusting in God doesn't guarantee success or victory. It doesn't protect us from suffering. Such trust doesn't even make the hurt go away, and it doesn't offer us longer life or fewer cavities. But it is in trusting God that we learn about a God who comes with us on every step of our journey. It is in surrendering our will and our control to God that we experience a healing God of accompaniment. For truly, our times are in God's hands, not ours, and our hope is in God's loving partnership as we journey together through the good times and the bad.

Psalm 31:9-16

It was late one night, and the young people in the church were having a party. There is no denying that things were a little rowdy. There is not much sense in pretending that the kids were not boisterous and dancing up a storm. It was, after all, a party. Suddenly, the door to the fellowship hall burst open and several churchfolk strode in and switched off the music with the crisp question, "Who's in charge here?"

The question really never did get answered, though the asking pretty much quelled the spirit of joy and rowdiness. However, it's a question worth asking and asking often. Who is, indeed, in charge here? In the church, for example, who is in charge? The pastor?

Mention that to most clergyfolk and the response will be a chuckle if not an outburst of laughter. Are the trustees in charge? Certainly, some would say so. Is the personnel committee in charge? Again, some would say so.

The truth of the matter, however, is that it's God who is in charge. Any other assertion of control is merely delusional. The problem encountered by people in all of life's settings is that delusion prevails. So many people act as though they are in charge; so many people live in delusion of power that real power never gets understood, utilized, or even acknowledged.

This psalm puts the matter straight in verse 14: "But I trust in you, O Lord; I say, 'You are my God.' My times are in your hand...."

How would the world look today if leaders both great and small, understood that the "times are in God's hands," not theirs? How would the church look today if clergy and layfolk alike understood that it was God who was in charge of the work and ministry?

The times are indeed in God's hands and the realization of this brings liberation. Released from the drive to control, people can reach in hope and healing. Freed from the need to win, community members can share and cooperate. Untethered from the necessity of determining the outcome, the people are released to discern God's leading rather than their own desires.

What a powerful community would emerge with God at the helm! What incredible witness could be given by a people not obsessed with being in charge! And finally, what a nation might be built if it were free of the will to power and given over instead to the justice and compassion of the holy one.

Psalm 32

Forgiveness is a beautiful thing. In the smog of anger and hurt that descends on the aftermath of human folly, forgiveness offers a new possibility. When people are locked in the circular frenzy of anger and hurt, forgiveness shatters the cycle. It is an almost comic understatement to suggest that those whose "transgressions" are forgiven are "happy!" Happy? Try ecstatic.

Forgiveness, it turns out, is tied closely to the notion of resurrection. After all, is it not forgiveness of sins that comes on the heels of an empty tomb? Is it not forgiveness that accompanied the thief to paradise? Is not forgiveness that gift shared in the Eucharist? To be forgiven is truly a holy experience. To forgive is to be in partnership with God.

Forgiveness is not just a mere dismissal of charges brought. Forgiveness involves an acknowledgment that wrong has been done. It doesn't gloss over or dismiss. Forgiveness is stark and clear about the reality that there is something that needs to be forgiven. You hurt my child? I have a basic right to strike back. You violate me? There is a visceral voice that justifies the call to even the score. Yet incredibly, forgiveness forfeits these legitimate claims to revenge. Forgiveness washes away the past and presents a clean slate; a new opportunity, a new beginning. Yes, forgiveness is a beautiful thing. Happy indeed are those whose transgressions are forgiven.

Forgiveness isn't just a one-time thing. The act of forgiveness is not an end in itself. It doesn't merely stop there. Forgiveness begs a response. It yearns for a flow and rhythm of grace that rushes from one forgiven person to another who needs what has just been received. Forgiveness forges pathways of new life and new beginnings. Forgiveness is a journey whose first steps are scary, tentative steps into the unknown. But once on the path, forgiveness strides forth with eyes open to the brokenness of the world.

This psalm is a shining link to the work of salvation in Christ Jesus, calling us to not only receive the gift of God's grace and forgiveness, but to turn and offer that same gift to others. It is this kind of offering that will make possible the building of what Reverend Martin Luther King Jr. referred to as the "beloved community."

Psalm 32

Forgiveness is difficult. Oh, with little things it can be done. Someone slips up and causes inconvenience. A little white lie here, a small mistreatment there, can be dismissed. But with the big things, it is not an easy matter. Who forgives betrayal in marriage?

Who forgives a deliberate attempt to hurt or wound? Who forgives a rapist or a murderer? Who forgives an invading, rampaging army? Who forgives us for the litany of wrongs that can be laid at our doorsteps?

Yet, forgiveness is the key to new life. Indeed, forgiveness is key to the continuation of life itself.

This psalm speaks to forgiveness from the point of view of confession. It is, in a sense, formulaic. First confession, then forgiveness, then a new beginning. The confession piece of this equation is critical. In fact, it is almost as though the deceit surrounding the wrongful act is worse than the act itself.

Isn't this true? It's bad enough that someone has been wronged, but when the perpetrator lies about the wrong and it is as though the infraction never took place, that's when things really get bad. If, however, the guilty party confesses — tells the truth — apologizes — forgiveness, and therefore a new beginning, becomes possible.

This dramatic process has been seen in the unfolding of the Truth and Justice Commissions in South Africa and in Guatemala after decades of horrible repression, violence, and murder. Those who committed the crimes came forward and told the truth. These were truths that staggar the imagination. Midnight kidnappings and murders, tales of death squads and massacres, and details too horrible to discuss here. Yet the truth was told.

In light of all this, it's distressing to note that many Protestant communities shy away from confession these days. In an effort to avoid "guilting" people, this most powerful and restorative process has been abandoned. One wonders if it might be retrieved. Deitrich Bonhoeffer felt that the Protestant church ought to return to the confessional for reasons quite similar to this.

The question that comes seems clear. What is the location of confession and forgiveness in the life of our nation? Where might this nation benefit from confession? Like any world power in history, the list here is long. From slavery to wars of empire, what would national confession look like? Where might our communities benefit from the truthfulness of confession? What truths might be told about homelessness and poverty? About racism and power?

And, of course, we cannot neglect our congregations. What healing truths might our churches tell? The list, of course, continues to narrow until at last we confront the one in the mirror.

Whether it is the sins of nations or the vagaries of one person, this psalm gets it right. Confession is good for the soul.

Psalm 33:1-12

"Praise befits the upright." This sounds right. It rolls off the tongue easily. Whether it's a "right and goodly thing to give thanks," or an improvised prayer of praise, we assume that praise is something that "upright" folks do on a regular basis.

The question that begs asking, however, is who exactly are the "upright"? More than two decades in parish ministry have shown this humble writer that the truly upright are rare creatures indeed. Are the "upright" self-identified? Does the usher at church know which ones are which? Do they wear T-shirts emblazoned with the words, "I'm Upright" on the front? And what does one have to do to become upright? Most folks hearing the word would identify the upright as the good folks who play by the rules. And as was just mentioned, these folks are rare. Most of us can claim our goodness in fits and spurts along life's highway and many of us bend or skirt rules from time to time; if not downright often!

Still it must be said, whoever and wherever they are, praise befits them. The Hebrew word that is translated as "upright" is *yashar*. The literal meaning of the word is indeed "upright." But there's another possibility that has to do with *yashar* referring to those who "stand up."

This presents us with an interesting twist in understanding. Rather than upright folks being the ones who follow the rules, what if they were the ones who actually stood up to be counted? This may well be someone who follows Torah. But it also would describe someone who stands up for Yahweh. By extension, these same upright people would stand up for the orphans and the widows, the poor and the marginalized. Upright people would stand up and speak out when the truth needed telling. Upright people would stand up for Jesus.

65

It brings to mind the old hymn, "Stand Up, Stand Up For Jesus!" One of the verses goes like this.

> *Stand up, stand up for Jesus; stand in his strength alone.*
> *The arm of flesh will fail you, you dare not trust your*
>   *own.*
> *Put on the gospel armor, each piece put on with prayer.*
> *Where duty calls or danger, be never wanting there.*

With its stirring melody and these lyrics, this is a wonderful song of praise and commitment to taking a stand. Indeed, praise does befit the "upright."

Psalm 34:1-8 (19-22)

The most fervent of prayers we can offer up to God is the living out of our lives in faithfulness. This sentiment was echoed in the writings of Saint Clement of Alexandria, a philosopher/theologian who died around 216 AD. Beyond the volumes of written prayers and liturgy that have piled up over the centuries, this simple dictum rings of authenticity. If our very lives are viewed as prayer, as an offering to God, what lives would we lead? If every action, every word, and every thought were understood to be prayer, things would change dramatically.

Could it be that the development of worship into segmented and compartmentalized sixty-minute chunks could have been a mistake? As one who writes materials for just such times, the thought is a bit daunting but worth considering. With people going to church on Sundays, church and the faith it is designed to nurture become relegated quite easily to the Sunday slot. Indeed, God help the pastor who strays much over the magic sixty-minute limit! We dare not, after all, let our faith interrupt the rest of our lives. What if church stopped being a location and reinvented itself as a way of being. In other words how is it that we can be the church together?

What if whole Christian communities could appropriate Paul's concept of being a "living offering"? (Romans 12:1). What if we abandoned worship as we know it and embarked upon lives that were a prayer being lifted up to God? What if we blessed the Lord "at all times," as the psalm suggests? What is suggested is really a seamless garment of faith. It is the ingestion of God's wonder into the body of Christ. What is hoped for is the rebirth of the church as each person begins to embrace the call to be praising God all the time, to be praying every day in every way with everything we do.

When we lift up the words, "O magnify the Lord with me," the question almost immediately arises. What will be used as a magnifier? The answer is simple to say, but will not be easy to do. The magnifier of God is to be our lives, lived in praise, wonder, and prayer. This way, it's easy to understand the notion of "tasting God," of experiencing God's wonder and goodness as we live out our lives as an act of prayer together. So it is these familiar and oft-said words could gain new life.

Psalm 34:1-10, 22

"I will bless the Lord at all times; his praise shall continually be in my mouth" (v. 1). Reading the first verse of this psalm gives pause, doesn't it? While any self-respecting Christian would hope that people would give praise "continually," the actual thought of ceaseless exaltation is a bit unsettling. Imagine someone who went around continually uttering shouts of praise and thanksgiving. No matter where they were or what they were doing, every word out of their mouths was about God and God's wonderful works. On the sidewalk, at the store, or in the dry cleaners: praise, praise, praise. Working, playing, or resting, such a person would never stop. It's one thing to do this on Sunday morning but at Starbucks? It's one thing to go to Bible study and exalt God's name, but do we really want to be around someone who does it while we're out to dinner? The truth of the matter is that such exuberance would be seen as zealotry in the eyes of most people. "Yes, yes, we know you love God, but could you please tone it down a bit?"

However, there could be another option. What if this psalm refers, not to a constant and potentially irritating God chatter, but to a deeper kind of praise? What if this psalm calls the reader to a life that is in itself an exclamation of praise? Instead of wagging tongues and idle talk, what if we were called to lives that truly witnessed to the depth of faith? Rather than going on and on about the greatness of God, what if we demonstrated God's wonder in lives of prayerful justice? It's true. There aren't too many people like this in our lives, but they do exist. It is said that Saint Francis exuded an aura of holiness. There are reports that being in the presence of Martin Luther King Jr. was like being in the midst of a living prayer. Some people have reported the powerful experience of being near great prophets like Daniel and Philip Berrigan. Each of these holy people did not merely speak of God's greatness. Instead, they used the gifts God had given them to display God's glory with their lives.

Imagine the power of a whole people living lives of praise and justice. Conjure up, if you can, a world blessed by the blessings of God through simple, holy people. Indeed, words of praise and exaltation should come continually from each person of faith. But clearly, such words are but half the equation.

Psalm 36:5-10

There is nothing quite so wonderful as someone you can trust. Most of us, if we're lucky, have had someone in our lives whom we can trust; someone who "has our back," through thick and thin; someone whose loyalty is never up for grabs. Maybe it's a parent or family member. Perhaps it's an old friend or a spouse. Whoever it is, there can be no doubt about it. There is nothing quite like knowing that there's someone who will not abandon us; someone who will never leave or betray our trust; someone who will be our rock in the storms of our lives.

The truth is, however, that even in the best of relationships, trust is betrayed. People are frail and weak, and they inevitably make mistakes or simply fail to show up when they are needed. This is, one imagines, why forgiveness is so basic to our faith. Without it, we would spiral down into chaos and destruction.

However, there is one whose love is "steadfast." There is someone who does not go away or abandon us; someone who is not fickle or frail. The identity of the "one," is obvious and rolls easily from the tongue. It is, however, another matter to really let go and trust in this "one," this God.

This is why a psalm like this one is so important. When people and their inconsistencies have left us wounded and prostrate, this psalm announces the wonder of God's "steadfast love." When the vagaries of life leave us empty and out of steam, this psalm bids us "take refuge" in the shadow of God's wings. When as humans we are exhausted and wasted from competition and striving, this psalm offers the ceaseless abundance of God's grace, comparing it to a "river of delights."

Once convinced of the fidelity of God, the rest of life takes on a different hue. Secure in God's "steadfast love," it becomes easier to risk and to take chances. Trusting in God's abundance allows us to lean into this sense of plenty in our own lives and relationships.

So it is that this is a psalm to take with us into our lives of prayer. Pray this psalm daily. Pray it when it seems like a joke. Pray it when cynicism rules the heart. Pray it when trust in people or institutions has failed. Pray it when loneliness creeps about the heart. Learn this psalm and carry it like a precious gift. Its promises, like the one it describes, are authentic and true.

Psalm 40:1-11

There is an unwritten law in lines at the local supermarket. The law states that if you change lines you will wait longer. No matter how carefully you check it out to see which line is shorter or how many things your neighbor has in their shopping cart, if you break ranks, if you step out of the line you're in and move to another line, it is decreed from somewhere that you will have a longer wait than if you had stayed in the line you first chose.

It's about patience — and it's no secret to anyone reading this that patience is in short supply in contemporary culture. Think about it. Wait just one second after the stoplight changes and someone behind you honks the horn. Walk down most any urban sidewalk and smell the rush and crush of getting wherever it is that has to be gotten in less time than is humanly reasonable. Hurry hurry, push

push, and God help anyone who makes us wait. Patience is indeed in short supply in our daily lives.

Yet, patience is one of the magic elixirs that propels life forward with greater ease and joy. It is the patient person who usually succeeds with troublesome children. It is the patient person who wins the confidence of others who are caught up in the stress of the moment. It is the patient person who awaits the right opportunities for a host of things in this life. Whether it's the right job or the right relationship, patience is a universal assistant.

The benefits of patience are no less present in our fumbling attempts to reach for the holy. The spiritually impatient — a description which fits many — fire off a quick prayer and wonder why God hasn't answered. The too-often operative expectation is that God will morph God's self to meet our expectations. How does that old Janis Joplin song go? "Oh, Lord, won't you buy me a Mercedes Benz...." If the new car doesn't come, and quick, faith is shaken.

But "waiting patiently for the Lord" offers 1,000 different benefits. Primary among them is that waiting usually requires quietude. We may not like it much, but there you are, waiting. And quietude makes it possible to hear things not usually audible in the daily rush of doing what we think is important.

What is it that patience brings? What comes when patience attends prayer? Perhaps it is patience that will provide; patience that will give space for God to "incline God's ear."

Psalm 41

Most of us love the church. Even when we struggle with its stumblings and imperfections, there is a piece of us that is at least fond of this home we have found. But love it or not, the truth is that Christian faith often loses credibility in its quixotic quest for niceness. Does this ring a bell? We try so hard to be nice. Our churches are full of nice people who smile and say, "Blessings on you," while all manner of behavior is quietly tolerated because, well, we're nice. It doesn't much matter what all is going on as long as we're ... nice. After all, we're supposed to love everyone, right? We're even supposed to love our enemies.

This facade of nice within our faith communities doesn't help us much in the long run. This is true for a few good reasons.

First, the truth is that we're really not all that nice. We're a broken people. We are sinful. While the world around us starves for both love and food, we feud and fight for power and control, and we don't, for the love of God, very often resemble the body of Christ.

The second reason that "nice" is not all that helpful is the fact that we live in a delusional kind of naïveté. It's the kind of attitude generated by the deadening ether of "I'm okay. You're okay." When we realize, as this psalm does, that none of us are really "okay," and that we actually do have enemies, we are a bit nonplussed. We thought nice would cover it all, but somehow it just doesn't.

The thought that there are enemies who actually sit and wonder when you will die (v. 5) is not pleasant. The idea that there are those who might gather mischief in their hearts (v. 6) against you just doesn't jive with our image of nice guy Jesus sitting with a lamb on his lap.

The hard reality is that there are enemies about in this life. They present themselves for a host of different reasons. But whatever the reason or the form they take, it is a fact of life, that most people have them.

In a kind of dumb-struck solidarity, we join with the psalmist in blessing those who care for the poor. After all, in these days who has more enemies than the poor? We lift up those who protect others, who won't give up someone to their enemies. And with this psalmist we pray for God's help when our enemies line up against us.

Perhaps, if we pray enough, the veneer of niceness will give way to the gritty presence of God's sustaining love. Could it be that in this love we would find the "moxy" to match our prayers with a kind of holy integrity? If so, prayer-tinged integrity would not only draw us closer to the God we seek, it just might also restore some of the credibility we squandered on nice.

Psalms 42 and 43

Thirst is a powerful thing. In a society where few ever go thirsty it's a difficult concept to embrace. Even though millions of people around the globe suffer from thirst, abundant and potable water is a blessing for most people in the United States. Think, though, about falling asleep with the mouth wide open. Then imagine awakening to a dry and parched tongue. The first thing that happens is a run to the bathroom for a quick glass of water. How good that water feels as it courses down the throat. This is a peek into the reality of thirst. It is a sense of absence of moisture, a dryness, a brittle parchment of flesh that yearns for water: This is thirst. This is the kind of thirst that humanity has for the holy.

There is a deep unmet yearning for a connection with God that is somehow built into the human spirit. It even visits those who deny God's existence. It is as though someone is in the desert without water for a number of days and stands swaying in the sun denying the existence of water. Within the human heart lives a desire for a refuge that represents a complete safety that is unavailable in most other corridors of life. There is a longing for something that completes and fulfills. This something is God.

God is missing in the lives of so many that it is not an easy thing to ponder. It is especially difficult when God seems to go missing in the lives of those who claim to believe in (him).

When tragedy strikes or bad luck turns terrible, believers wonder about this God of refuge. When injustice rears its contorted face or when implacable systems quash the human spirit, those who claim God find themselves despairing of God's presence.

Yet, it is precisely into these fractured moments that God reaches to find us. It is into the turmoil of brokenness and grief that God's healing wonder seeps. This is why the psalmist does not abandon prayers of praise, even though the enemy is at the gates. This is why the trust and hope in the holy is never withdrawn, even when oppression grinds the soul into dust and tears.

There will be moments, days, perhaps even years when it feels as though God has, as the young folk say, "blown us off." But it is in this darkness, in the crisis time, in the midst of mourning that the dawn of the holy shines forth.

It is not for nothing that down the years we learn that it is only through the cross that we find the resurrection.

Psalm 45:1-2, 6-9

Leaders of all stripes have always had sycophants in abundance to sustain their delusion of power. Doting tongues to puff up the king are nothing new. From Elizabethan jesters to plaster-faced, neck-tied staffers in oval offices, it seems a constant theme. But here we find a caveat of sorts. Sure, the king is a "handsome man." Let us be clear, however, about where real power is to be found.

It's God who anoints, and as it turns out, God has a few qualifications in mind. The scepter is to be one of equity. That is, equal justice, equal opportunity, equal rights, and here's the hobgoblin in the mix, equal distribution of the material resources of the land.

This isn't all. The king is to be a "lover of righteousness." It's one thing to go on record as one approving of righteousness. It's yet another to love it. This love implies a passion beyond intellectual assent. This love asserts a depth of commitment; a sense of intimacy connected with righteousness — an understanding that this isn't a game being played here.

Delving into this psalm begs the question, "How do our contemporary leaders measure up to God's qualifications?" Is the scepter of our current leadership one of equity? Look across the landscape of our nation. Is equal justice available to everyone, or is it more available to those who can afford it? Is there equal opportunity in education and employment? Are equal rights available to everyone?

It's safe to say that the answer to the above questions is a resounding "No." With African Americans making up the vast majority of our prison population, and only a small fraction of our national population, equal justice is reduced to the level of meaningless rhetoric. With our public schools languishing for lack of funding and support, the notion of equal opportunity evaporates. And in a post 9/11 environment of fear, equal rights and other civil protections fall to the ground and are trampled by the boots of "national security."

73

But enough of all this. The real question still goes unasked. Where does this leave a biblical people? If, as scripture and circumstances suggest, the king is not following the dictates of God, what are the worshipers of God to do? The options are legion indeed, and this space will halt just short of specific suggestions.

Only this: Real faith is not silent. Deep faith is not inactive. Committed faith will not permit injustice and oppression to continue unabated. Authentic faith knows, finally, that God is not mocked.

Psalm 45:10-17

Here is a woman who is given over to a new "Lord." The advice is clear, even curt. To paraphrase a favorite film of years gone by, it amounts to this. "Honey, you ain't in Kansas anymore!" The family and focus of old no longer applies in the courts of this new Lord. It's time to deal with the reality that is right in front of us. Certainly the psalm here could be read through twenty-first-century eyes, which take a dim view of women being portrayed as chattel. With that perspective, who could argue?

However, if one looks past the almost irresistible impulse to judge ancient text from contemporary context, there is a larger message to be heard. Could it be that each person, regardless of the path they take, comes to a point where it's important to acknowledge that things have changed? Whether it's the young virgin moving into the household of her new lord, or a Christian community moving into a new century, isn't it important to acknowledge that the landscape is different?

If the young woman who is now under the charge of a new lord continues to act as though her father and her family are her reality, it seems reasonable to assume that things may not go well for her. Similarly, a church community that has moved into a new cultural era needs to acknowledge that things have changed.

It's like the person who grew up in a rain forest. Living in an environment of constant moisture and dampness, it's natural to dress in a way that makes it more comfortable to live in that part of the world. But if one moves to the desert and continues to dress as though he was still in the rain forest, a few eyebrows might be raised in concern, or even mockery.

Yes, the call that emerges today is one for awareness. It's important for everyone to be aware of location, of context, and to not be lulled into thinking that where we used to be is where we are now. It's a word for us as individuals and certainly a word for us as Christian community.

Psalm 46

There is a growing and dangerous form of Christian faith spreading around the land. It goes by a number of names, and it is both insidious and unhelpful. One name for it is the "Gospel of Prosperity." The "Gospel of Prosperity" is based on a fundamental understanding of faith as transactional. That is, if you are good and if you believe in God, then God will reward you. The reward, in many cases, is monetary, but it includes general well-being. If you're good, if you believe, then God will take care of you and bad things won't happen.

This is a shallow faith. It is shallow because it serves only as long as luck lasts. Sooner or later, something less than pleasant happens to everyone. A parent dies, a spouse cheats, a friend betrays; everyone experiences these things sooner or later. If your faith in God is tied to how well God treats you, then poof! Faith evaporates when suffering begins.

A deep faith knows, as does this psalm, that faith in God is not an insurance policy against suffering nor a guarantee of a successful life. "God is a very present help *in* trouble," not a get-out-of-jail-free card.

It is precisely in the midst of our troubles that God comes most wonderfully and most fiercely. It is that presence that finds us in our sorrow and says, "Be still, and know that I am God." It is that presence that walks with us through our grief and through the dangers and toils we will face. It is that presence that pulls us into the future tense of glory.

There is also a deeper and more mystical truth that involves the ways in which suffering actually deepens us. Like metals refined

75

in the fire, we, too, are often strengthened by trials through which we walk. A parishioner going through a painful and nasty divorce had no way of seeing what might come in the years ahead. Yet meeting with him some years later, it was striking to note the depth and power this man's life had assumed. Moreover, it was moving to see how healing had indeed come to him.

The "Gospel of Prosperity" is easy. It's appealing. It sells lots of books. But in the end it simply does not serve. Instead, we are called to a God who is more than an insurance policy. We are called by a God who accompanies us on every step of the journey. Through it all, God is with us.

Psalm 46

"Be still and know that I am God."

How difficult it is to be still. The world in which we live conspires to make of us a blur as we rush about doing all the things we feel called to do. Indeed, it is difficult to be still. Today, the average worker in the American work force puts in fifteen to twenty more hours a week than a worker did a generation ago. Today, the demands of parenting and community are overwhelming as many find themselves also caring for aging parents. Being still? Sounds nice, but when would that happen? During sleep?

People are so busy that there is a new church demographic arising in families who actually make it to church about once a month. These folks self-identify as church members. They give financially and sometimes even serve in the ministry of the church. But all they have time for is to attend church once a month.

We are experiencing an epidemic of busy-ness. All the labor saving devices showered upon us only seem to make us busier still. Computers that once lived on our desks now follow us around for use in our laps. At home, in the cafe, in the car, and even on vacation we cannot seem to stop moving. Cell phones have turned to smart phones so that email and text messages can follow us wherever we go, there is even talk of communication devices that can be surgically implanted near one's ear!

Be still, and know that I am God. It would seem that it's the stillness part that is the challenge for us. In an ever-quickening world, how do church leaders help people slow down and even stop for a little while? As the pace picks up and everyone sprints a little faster, is there a way that the Christian community can invite people into a stillness where God waits?

The answer to the question is, of course, "Yes." But getting there is still a challenge. The first thing, perhaps, is to utter a call to stillness. Even if it's only ten minutes a day, everyone can find this little window to simply stop and be still. Once the call is uttered, perhaps it might be possible to build stillness into the worship life of the community. Quakers are good at this, but most Protestants fill their worship with noise and chatter. What if a worship service carved out five whole minutes for silence and stillness?

"Be still, and know that I am God." These are admittedly modest proposals. Perhaps the readers will have their own ideas? Whatever happens, it is important, even critical for leaders to help the people slow down, stop, and claim the stillness where knowledge of God begins.

Psalm 47

Reading this psalm, one can almost hear the hip-hop beat. "Clap your hands all you people! Shout to God with loud songs of joy!" Is everyone ready? It's time to dance! It's that deep, loud, bass rhythm that sets off the car alarms as the car cruises down your block. It's that almost primal urge to simply move to the rhythms of joy and wonder. This has the makings of a praise party. It is a time where God's people gather to revel in the sheer joy of claiming their heritage as God's own.

This is worship on a profound level. When the restraints are dropped and the heart is opened to God's transforming power, it is indeed time to clap the hands. When we shed the narrowness of our own viewpoints and embrace the sacred vision of God, the time has come to dance.

Yes, this is worship that is deep. It is an intimate and holy connection. But if it stops here it's only a party. If it doesn't go further than this, it sputters out and tires as surely as the dancers will in half an hour or so.

This worship, this hand-clapping, foot-stomping, shouting out to God is the first step in truly faithful worship. Real worship leads the people out of the sanctuary and into lives of justice and hope. The prophets are clear in this area. Isaiah asks us in chapter 58 about the kind of "fasting" that God wants.

Amos writes,

> *I hate, I despise your festivals, and I take no delight in your solemn assemblies. Even though you offer me your burnt offerings and grain offerings, I will not accept them; and the offerings of well-being of your fatted animals I will not look upon. Take away from me the noise of your songs; I will not listen to the melody of your harps. But let justice roll down like waters, and righteousness like an ever-flowing stream.*
> — Amos 5:21-24

Yes, let's stomp our feet and shout for joy! Let's join this psalmist in praising God, but please, please, let it not simply stop there.

Psalm 47

"Clap your hands, all you people! Shout to God with loud shouts of joy!" What images of fun and frolic this paints in the imagination. Behind the shouting and the clapping is an old New-Orleans-style jazz band. All around the band are daisy chains of people wrapped arm and arm, caught in the throes of dance and song. It is exuberance and wonder, joy and clarity, all bound up in one powerful package.

Such a scene warms us. We long for such unrestrained expression and wonder vaguely why that is so difficult for us. Bound up, as we are, in cords of appropriateness and process, it's difficult to let it all out in one whoop of ecstasy, isn't it? In fact, many of us look askance at ecstatic expressions of faith.

The question begs the asking. Why is that? Why are ecstatic utterances of faith shoved to the margins of the less than serious? Why is the whoop and holler of this psalm something not witnessed in many of our worship services today? Is it because we are afraid of emotion? Is it because we shudder at what feels like a loss of control? Or is it that, down deep, we really are not in agreement with the notion that it is God, and not us, who is in charge?

There is perhaps a bit of risk in saying so, but the answer must be, "Yes" to all three questions.

First, many of us are afraid of our emotions. We live in a tightly controlled environment that shoves intimacy and extremity of feelings neatly out of sight. We paper it over, of course, with language about boundaries and, once again, appropriateness. So tightly wound are we that it is nearly impossible to cut through our defenses to the heart, which is where God operates.

Second, is control. We are a culture of control freaks. We have a need to be in charge. From the stage of world politics to the color of our cars, we want to believe that we have made a choice. A stroll down a supermarket aisle reveals the pernicious nature of this obsession. Choice. Choosing makes us feel powerful and in charge. If God is totally in charge, then what of our freedom to choose? If it is God who rules the nations, then what of *our* input? This leads to the fearsome notion that we may not *want* God to be in charge. Could this idolatrous drive to unseat God be the primary source of our muted, unenthusiastic praise? It conjures up images of the faint-hearted applause at a wedding where few approve of the choice of spouses.

Our journey to control and finally to unseat God can be seen in the destruction of our ecology and in our ongoing maintenance of an arsenal that can undo God's entire creation in a hellish flash of fire. If we can destroy it, are we not greater than the creator?

But the song persists. Through the mire of our faithlessness comes the ancient song. "Clap your hands, all you people! Shout to God with loud shouts of joy!" It is a harmony that will not retreat. The strains of the melody lift up the heart. The rhythms of the drums unchain the soul, and through tightly controlled emotions, through the compulsion to be in charge, comes the unrestrained wonder of knowing, simply, that God is God. Indeed, it is God who is in charge after all. So pick up that trumpet and blow. Sing out to the Lord. Celebrate the one of glory who is our creator and our ruler, our Savior and our sovereign.

Psalm 47

Psalm 47 conjures memories of long ago rock concerts where throngs of jubilant young people roared their delight in music that reached for a new day of understanding, peace, and gentleness. Fond as those recollections may be, they are but a starting point for the celebration entered into in this psalm. This is a total declaration of praise. It is a dance of sparkling clarity that claims God's power over all other powers. Clapping hands, shouting voices, and blaring trumpets may move the blood and excite the passions, but they are nothing compared to the wonders of this God!

This God gave us the dirt under our feet! This God gave us the gift of our heritage; our connectedness through the generations! This God rules over the nations! The greatness of this creator king staggers our ability to describe or define. All that is left is the ecstasy of a holy noise. Stomp the feet, clap the hands, dance in celebration, and let trumpets blast the high note. It is an unrestrained improvisation of joy! Let the dance begin!

If such an outbreak of praise were to happen in a church today, what would it look like? What would it sound like? What would it feel like? And more to the point, where would it lead? If the declaration of praise and worship were so complete that there was not confusion, what might happen among God's people? What kinds of faithfulness might erupt from such a celebration?

If the church could claim the sovereignty of God with overwhelming power, what mighty things might happen? As the church looks into the clouds on this Ascension Day, what is it that God is calling for on the ground?

Stop for just a moment. Breathe deeply. Release the constraints of the so-called "real world." Look deep inside and find that new rhythm of praise. Bring the hands together. Tap the feet and give your body over to the music of God's transforming power. Our

God reigns! There is nothing that cannot be done! The lame can walk! The deaf can hear! The oppressed shall be liberated, and the poor shall receive their due. This is God's time. This is God's world. And we, thanks be to our Lord Jesus Christ, are God's people!

May the prayers from our hearts call us to faithfulness. And may this faithfulness lead us where God would have us go.

Psalm 48

It is not an easy thing to grasp something greater than ourselves. With our own frailties and limitations we see, as Paul reminds us (1 Corinthians 13:9), only a part of the picture. By our own make up, we can never really grasp the totality of creation or the vastness of the universe. And when we try to think about the one who created it all, the senses are drowned in the stormy waters of incredulity. Call it what you will, God, Yahweh, the prime mover, the name matters little as we stand in slack-jawed awe before this mystery, this wonder that we name as God.

This psalm attempts to sketch out some of this grandeur as it describes the response of the "assembled kings" to God's glorious city. Consider our own response to things beyond ourselves. Few, if any, can summon up the wisdom or the courage to step into things unknown, let alone the vast mystery of God's holiness. Naturally, fear comes first. Panic, trembling, and a deep incredible pain accompany the reaction to those who attend on God's glory.

In a time such as this when populations are manipulated and managed through the use of fear, this response to God is instructive. It teaches us, first, that there is a vast difference between governing authorities and God. Though kings and leaders have always tried to abscond with God's power and authority, they still tremble in the Lord's presence. It is to our own peril that we mortals forget this difference. Governments and kings may rule here on the ground, but God alone is creator and redeemer. Nations bristle with weapons and squander their wealth on warfare, but God alone possesses power over life and death. The learning here is to understand in our deepest self that it is to God and God alone that we owe our final allegiance.

81

The second reading has to do with moving beyond our first fearful response to God's wonder and glory. So often, we get mired down in the goo of our fear and expend our life's energy spinning our wheels in the muck of terror. But if we can let go of fear, if we can release our death grip on our own inner terror, we can stop and "ponder" God's "steadfast love" for us.

What a thing it is to claim! That the creator of the universe loves ... us! And yet there it is. Beyond the spectacle of glory, beyond our fearful living lies God's beautiful, inestimable love for us. Indeed, with the psalmist, this is something worth pondering.

Psalm 50:1-6

How do we feel about judgment? Buoyed up by thin interpretations of New Testament scripture, our relativistic culture has decided that we don't feel good about it. Truthfully, no one likes to be judged. We especially don't like to be judged by other people. But here, we're talking about a higher power. Here, we come face-to-face, not with judgmental finger wagging zealots, but with God.

God calls upon the people with some rather dramatic fanfare. The "perfection of beauty," does not come subtly or quietly, but with a "devouring fire" in the lead and a "mighty tempest" surrounding [him].

It turns out that this is the real deal, and we are called to receive God's judgment upon us. Of course there are several possible reactions to all this. Some might strengthen an already healthy sense of denial and say, "Bring it on." Others, already wracked with self-doubt and insecurity, might simply quake where they are and wait, frozen in abject terror. Still others might get lost trying to weigh a lifetime of moments and decisions made long ago.

The summons issued in these verses implies a coming one-time thing. It could be referred to as the "big bang" of judgment. Indeed, the text suggests this, but what if God's judgment doesn't cohere to our sense of time? What if God's judgment isn't waiting around for some unknown, unmentioned appointed moment? What if God's judgment is already here? More than that, what if God's judgment is ongoing? An always thing?

How would things change if judgment were not off in some vague future, but here and now? Imagine the politician who is keenly aware that God is not only watching, but also judging his or her actions. Conjure up a vision of a church with a crystalline awareness that God is very much present and very concerned with how we are representing God's interests.

This God who summons us to hear the indictment against us is the same God who walks with us each and every moment of our lives. This God who is about to announce judgment is the same God who has numbered the hairs on our heads, who has known us, even in our mother's wombs. And, as almost anyone can tell you, judgment from someone who knows you is a lot tougher than the opinion of a stranger.

Yes, this God who comes accompanied by fire and storm to announce judgment upon us doesn't have a real big commute. So maybe it would be a good idea to try to shape up now. Where would you begin? Where would our church communities begin? Where should our nation begin? Because God's not merely on his way. God's here now. And God's judgment is an always thing.

Psalm 50:1-8, 22-23

Ask someone who doesn't go to church what it is that they don't like about church. Ask anyone. In fact, ask several people. Invariably they will say that they don't like all that judgment stuff. If they're talking about judgmental people, then who can blame them? No one wants to step into a community and find the wagging finger of judgment pointed in their direction. But on the other hand, if it's judgment in general that these folks are trying to avoid, that might be worth a moment's consideration.

Maybe it's a hangover from the "I'm okay, you're okay days," but people really don't want to deal with this concept, especially if it's God who's doing the judging. But there it is. Throughout our scriptural tradition we find God as judge. Thankfully, it's God who gets to do that, because frankly, we're not up to the task.

If we are allowed to do the judging, the whole enterprise is doomed. We humans judge according to silly things like race, gender, or religion. We even stoop to judging people by their clothes or other meaningless preferences. But God isn't concerned with our trivial and shallow issues. God will judge us ... God *is* judging us now by the way we love one another, by the way we care for the planet God gave us to look after, and by the way we care for the poor.

The bottom line here really isn't about judgment itself. It's about being accountable. Those who would wiggle into a judgment-free zone in life also wish to escape from accountability. We are, simply put, accountable for our actions. We write this fundamental principle into our human laws. In our social context we "covenant" not to kill one another, unless of course it's sanctioned by the state. Then it's okay. But in our streets and neighborhoods we try to live by this covenant of not harming or stealing from one another. Our laws provide accountability measures to help assure that the rest of us can live in safety and relative comfort.

The same is pretty much true with God. We have covenant with God, who is our God, and we are (his) people. If we violate the covenant we are held accountable, not by the local police and justice system, but by the one with whom we have made the agreement.

At the end of the day, accountability is a pretty good thing. It works in our social arrangements, and it works in our relationship with God.

So the next time someone tells you they don't like church because of this judgmental God stuff, try talking to them about accountability.

Psalm 51:1-12

Once in a while, it occurs to us that we can be real stinkers. Occasionally, it dawns on us that we are serial sinners. The hard truth is that we just can't quit. And in those rare moments we stand convicted, and we feel it. Is it guilt? Shame? Self-loathing? All these emotions, long banished by our feel-good era, come to us if ever we get in touch with the basic fact of our own brokenness. "Denial," as the man said, "ain't a river in Egypt."

It is one of these times of brutal self-honesty that the psalmist portrays for us here. The utterance begins with a cry for mercy. Then comes a no-holds-barred confession. If we feel that scripture mirrors our own lives, even a little, this reading hits awfully close to home.

"I know my transgressions, and my sin is ever before me." This is, of course, true. We do know what we have done wrong and to whom we have done it. Most of the time we plaster it over with denial or flimsy justification. Some of us even buy the cultural lie that "I'm okay, and you're okay." Well, friends, we're not okay. We are sinners.

The beauty of this psalm lies in the clarity and depth of this awareness. The cry for forgiveness becomes, in this context, crystalline in its authenticity. "Blot out my transgressions, wash me thoroughly from my iniquity and cleanse me from my sin." This is the voice of someone who knows that they have done wrong. A young man sharing with his pastor about his adulterous behavior says that he feels queasy, almost sick to his stomach, as he realizes the depth of the pain and hurt he has caused as a result of his thoughtless and selfish actions. That queasy feeling is what the old gospel song calls a "sin-sick soul."

And the cure, another song declares, is "Doctor Jesus." The cure is the acceptance of God's forgiving grace, which results in a "clean heart and a new and right spirit within" (v. 10). The questions for us, then become: How often do we center our hearts in prayer before God? When was the last time we stripped ourselves bare and made a complete confession of our sins? How often do we "get real" and ask God's forgiveness for those sins?

Whether we are able to do this daily or once a year, a good way to begin is to sit down in a quiet place and read this psalm over five times quietly. It's a good way to start.

Psalm 51:1-12

Forgiveness — it's the Christian buzzword. We talk about it a lot. It is bandied about more than almost any other Christian idea, but it is seldom practiced. It is like the bicycle that sits in the garage and is never ridden. Yet the truth is that forgiveness is amazing. If you've received it, you know. There is nothing quite like it, and this psalm endeavors to claim that turf.

This isn't the forgiveness that accompanies everyday living, though we need that as well. This is deep. This is forgiveness that greets unthinkable wrongs. This is mercy that can come only to the undeserving.

Most people, in the wake of a misdeed, try to wiggle out of consequences that loom on the horizon. Not so in this case. Here, we have someone who has come to grips with the depth of their brokenness.

"I know my transgression, and my sin is ever before me ..." (v. 3).

From the quicksand of denial, this writer rises and makes this simple and clear confession. "I messed up, God. I really did it this time, and I need your forgiveness." How often do we see such candor? Instead of this simple, contrite plea, we are too often hosed down with self-righteous posturing and what has come to be known as "plausible denial." In other words, it doesn't have to be true, it just has to seem believable.

Here in this incredible psalm is a lesson that pierces the fact of our sinfulness and calls us to confession. Dietrich Bonhoeffer, one of the most powerful martyrs and theologians of the twentieth century, felt that the Protestant community needed to reclaim the confessional. In his underground seminary in war-time Germany, he taught students to hear one another's confessions, understanding the power of this kind of clarity and truthfulness.

Bonhoeffer was on to something. In our Protestant tradition we have trivialized confession to the point where it feels like we're in the interrogation room with God, admitting the wrongs we've done. But it's more than that. Authentic confession isn't about admission of errors and missteps, it's about truth-telling (v. 6a). It's about coming clean and saying the truth, not merely about what we've done, but about what is in our hearts, and finally, it is about where our true allegiance is to be found.

When we enter into this kind of confession, the healing is profound. We experience what feels like a new spirit and a clean heart (v. 10). We find that like God's grace, forgiveness is indeed amazing.

Psalm 51:1-17

It may not seem like a big deal, but has anyone noticed that confession has fallen out of favor in a lot of churches these days? From coast to coast, confessional prayer has slipped quietly from worship services across the land. The reasons proffered for this are that clergy don't want to make people feel guilty. "We don't," as one pastor put it, "do guilt." Certainly, guilt used as a manipulative tool to keep the pew sitters in line is not a good thing. But guilt in and of itself is not a bad thing at all. Like fear, guilt is a primal human emotion.

Fear is a good thing when it causes the Neanderthal to flee from the saber-toothed tiger. Guilt, too, can be a good thing. It can inform the guilty one that a given course of action isn't a good thing. Guilt can cause us to stop what we're doing and think things over. Maybe that twinge you feel as you steal just a few dollars from the petty cash jar at work is trying to tell you something?

Yet in our "I'm okay, you're okay" world we seldom want to deal, not only with guilt, but with the basic human propensity to sin. Church circles are abuzz with the notion that we are all good, which is nice and keeps things on the pleasant side during coffee hour, but it is not accurate. A simple look at the newspaper will reveal our brokenness and our sinful leanings as a people. It is not popular these days, but it is true.

This psalm is a stunning exercise, not only in dealing with guilt, but in calling all the faithful to new levels of self-awareness and honesty. "I know my transgression. My sin is ever before me...." This is confession. And it is, in spite of the power of cliché, good for the soul. These words go to the heart of our need to come clean before God and one another. At the end of the day we are not, in fact, all okay. Collectively, we lie, cheat, steal, betray, oppress, and murder. And that, as the man says, is on a good day!

The church needs confession. Its people need confession. The church needs to foster honesty and openness about the times when we go astray so that we can avail ourselves of God's forgiveness and grace, and perhaps this psalm is a good place to begin.

Psalm 51:1-17

As this Lenten season begins, it might be a good thing to think deeply about confession. This psalm goes to the heart of the matter as the writer comes clean. "I know my transgressions, and my sin is ever before me." In a world of believable deniability where taking responsibility for our mistakes and missteps is not common, this writing goes straight to the heart. So many of us are like the adolescent boy who gets caught breaking a window. And this applies to people from the lowest to the highest stations in our culture. The first impulse is self-righteous denial. "I didn't do it!" After it becomes painfully obvious that, in fact, the boy did break the window, the fallback is "it's not my fault!" Finally, when all else fails, the boy accepts responsibility and takes on some chores to pay for the new window to replace the one he broke.

The psalmist speaks the truth. If we peel away our own layers of denial and self-delusion, we know what we have done wrong. We are aware of the damage we have done and the hurt we have caused. And with our "I'm okay, you're okay" pop culture notwithstanding, each person knows down deep that they are not — in fact — okay.

It is here that confession emerges, not as a finger wagging, shame-inducing process, but as the beginning of God's healing plan for each person. In confession, truth is told. Truth about actions taken and not taken; truth about words said and words left unsaid. In confession truth is told about what is found deep in the heart. And like the psalmist, as we also come clean before God, abundant healing and mercy is offered.

When truth is told, the dodging and defensiveness can disappear. When all is laid out on the table and truth is offered, not merely to God, but to the self, the wounds inflicted can begin to heal. When all the layers of denial and falsehood disappear it becomes clear that God isn't out to get us. God isn't looking for us to slit our throats in guilt at "his" feet. No. All God desires is the truth; the truth that is already known to God but hidden in our pride and arrogance from our own eyes.

All that God desires, it turns out, is a broken and contrite heart so that healing can begin. Would that everyone, from government leaders to parish councils, could take this step into truth-telling and confession. For if we are all honest, we know our sins all too well, and they are ever before us as we enter this season.

Psalm 52

Schoolyard bullies populate the memory of a lot of people. Even if the blows and the taunting did not come specifically in a given direction, memories remain. Pushing, shoving, horrible taunts, and even violence were hurled at hapless youngsters whose only crime was to walk meekly down the hallway past a bully who sensed an opportunity.

Unfortunately, bullies never seem to go out of vogue. Each generation of schoolchildren must endure the loud-mouthed vituperative antics of those who "boast of mischief done against the godly." The problem, though, rarely stops at the school playground. Young bullies grow into adult bullies unless someone stands and puts a stop to the abuse. The voice of this psalm is the voice of just such a one.

This voice fires a salvo back at the "evil-doer," which in schoolyard lingo might be heard as, "Oh, yeah? You just wait! God's gonna get you!" Though this tone resonates through the psalm, there is a deeper truth running like a vein of silver through this text. And that is that "God is not mocked. You will reap what you have sown" (Galatians 6:7). In the hot, flushed moments of seeming victory when abusive power asserts itself with violence, the temptation to gloat and crow is overwhelming. But as Martin Luther King Jr. said, "The arc of the universe is long, and it bends toward justice."

Whether it is a schoolyard bully, or a war-making nation, God is not mocked. What is sown will indeed be reaped. From the corridors of power to rural backwaters and dark urban alleys, the seeds that have been sown will sprout.

The harvest of this crop will be great. God's wondrous and powerful hand will reach through the vista of our own story and establish justice. The trust placed in God, even in the face of such evil, is not misplaced. It is a source of power and strength, a well whose waters never run dry. This is why such a one can laugh in the face of the "evildoer." This is why the weakest ones will ultimately triumph. And it is why good, decent, righteous people must never remain silent in the face of a schoolyard bully, regardless of where the schoolyard is located or what the bully looks like.

Psalm 62:5-12

The storybooks of our faith are full of heroes and martyrs who have insisted on the sovereignty of God in their lives. From the biblical account of Stephen succumbing to a hail of stones right up to the assassination of Archbishop Oscar Romero, these stories populate the landscape of Christendom. Yet, in our contemporary lives we set ourselves strangely apart from them. The Greek word, of course, is *martus*, meaning "witness."

Today, however, martyrdom has been shunted aside as something best dealt with on a psychologist's couch. Instead of seeing a martyr as a heroic witness to our faith, contemporary sensibilities have identified it as a diagnosis. Having dispensed with such uncomfortable notions, the idea of standing resolutely for something fades to black in our television-screen consciousness.

It's true. Those who insist on maintaining God as their "rock and their salvation," who place their hope and their trust in God alone, are usually a stubborn lot, and stubborn people don't often fare well in the mainstream of reality. Indeed, it's been said that if Stephen were a little more agreeable, slightly more malleable, that he might well have been spared. Indeed, if Archbishop Romero had tempered his homilies against the death squads he, too, might still be serving Eucharist, instead of lying prone amidst the wine and the host.

Yet, in all this it must be said that ours is such a faith. This psalm lays it on our doorstep and dares us to step over it on our way into the rest of our lives. We read that God is our deliverer;

that our trust is to be in God and no one else, and carrying on, we learn that power belongs to God. Not to guns or government, not to market forces or police forces, but to God and God alone. Extreme, you say? Perhaps. But such a sentiment hardly exists in isolation within our tradition. Check out the first of the Ten Commandments for starters.

For us this is no easy walk in the park. In the midst of lives where a host of entities compete for our loyalty, how do we wait upon "God alone"? While we may not wish to put our confidence in extortion or robbery, it doesn't take a rocket scientist to look around and see that much of the world does. What, we are left to ask, is a Christian to do? How are we to place our trust in God and God alone? How do we live fully and faithfully before our God?

Perhaps, as it has throughout our history, the answer begins in community. Maybe faithfulness starts in the context of love and trust in the congregation. Could it be that relationships formed in faith and lived out in covenant are where our faithfulness to God begins? It would seem that the answer needs to be, "Yes."

Do such leanings leave us out on a limb? Probably, but if the branch breaks, at least we know where our prayers will be going.

Psalm 63:1-8

At the core of our faith is the basic tenet that we must surrender ourselves to God. In a culture such as ours, the idea of self-surrender is tantamount to insanity. In the world in which most of us must work and live, victory is the maxim. We are called to win. In fact, even a casual observation of our national leaders today will reveal the rigid insistence upon victory even as they are swallowed up in defeat. This culture insists that each person must put himself first. The message is ubiquitous. From saturation advertising to the therapeutic couch, we are constantly told that we must take care of ourselves first, that we must love ourselves before we can love others. It is the air we breathe.

Into this narcissistic smog comes the beauty of this psalm. Into the frenetic pace and cynicism of daily life comes the pure, vulnerable wonder of one who seeks God. It is more, however, than simple seeking. This is an acknowledgment of the need for the holy. "My soul thirsts for you, my flesh faints for you as in a dry and weary land where there is no water."

In this insane and twisted world, the soul longs for the foundation stone of the creator. God's faithful love, we hear, is better than life. God's presence satisfies the soul like a banquet satisfies the belly.

This psalm moves to the rhythms of self-surrender and exposes the beauty of putting God — rather than ourselves — at the center of our lives. This is a psalm worth praying every day. These words are worth committing to memory and saying them over and over again. These words should be allowed to sculpt the spirit and shape the soul.

This psalm conjures up the old hymn, "Jesus calls us from the tumult of our life's wild restless sea; day by day his sweet voice soundeth, saying, 'Christian, follow me.' " We are called, both as individuals, and as people to turn from the "tumult," to rise above the craziness, and to give ourselves fully and completely to the wonder of God's incredible love.

This psalm calls us to lives of prayer and worship. It places our need for God in sharp focus and bids us turn from this "dry and weary land" to the life-giving waters of God's Holy Spirit.

Psalm 65

There are two fundamental theories that govern our human existence. In actuality there are likely many more than two, but for our purposes here there are two. The first is the *Theory of Scarcity*. That is the idea that human existence is governed by the core belief that there is never really enough of anything. It's as though the stuff of life was reduced to a pie, and we believed with all our hearts that there were no more pies to be had and that the quality of our lives was to be determined by how much of this pie we could obtain.

This *Theory of Scarcity* is the basic mode in which our culture operates. Everyone spends their life energy scrambling for their piece of the pie, desperate in the belief that there is only so much.

The result, of course, is conflict and strife in every corner of our human reality.

The other theory is the *Theory of Abundance*. This theory operates on the core belief that not only is there enough for everyone, there is, in fact, an abundance of all that is needed for life to be full and joyful. A world duped into believing in the theory of scarcity can hardly imagine the concept of abundance as a chosen life assumption.

One basic characteristic of the *Theory of Abundance* is the presence of grateful and thankful hearts. Imagine it just for a moment. If the world is perceived and experienced as a place where our needs will be more than met, how can anything but gratitude be expressed? On the other hand, if the world is a place where there is never enough, and our lives are characterized by struggle and strife just to get a piece of the pie, then it is not gratefulness, but rather a hardness of heart that prevails.

Psalm 65 lifts up the spirit of the *Theory of Abundance*, and names it as God's choice for all creation. This psalm assumes the reality of God's grace and mercy. It leans with trust into the notion that "we shall be satisfied with the goodness ..." of God's house. Read this psalm carefully and let the imagination roam to a world where the *Theory of Abundance* is the operative paradigm. Failing that, perhaps we might imagine a church that lives that way.

Psalm 65

Every morning when sleep leaves and waking comes there is cause for praising God. Caught up, as we are, in the currents and eddies of our lives, this is easy to forget. This wonderful psalm is a reminder. God's bounty and abundance spill into our lives like waters over a causeway. God's delight in creation explodes in a million different colors. In every moment there is reason to give God praise.

Once, when visiting a church out of town, I heard the pastor call for the people to adopt an "attitude of praise." What a wonderful concept this man offered his congregation. Usually when we speak of attitude it has a bad connotation. "That woman has a real attitude." But what if our attitude was one of continual praise of God? As my fingers wander over my keyboard in the process of writing this, I marvel at how they work. Praise God! I glance across the room and see my family, reading and studying alongside me. Praise God! As a pastor I have the high privilege of walking with people down the corridors of their lives. It is an unbelievable gift. Praise God!

What would be the litany of praise that would articulate your life? What, aside from the obvious gifts of creation around us, would you list as you adopt your attitude of praise? The joyful chatter of Christian community? The precious gift of useful work? A chance to walk on the beach?

How different the world might be if praise became the medium with which we painted our lives. Rather than ambition or pride, turn to praise. Instead of greed or anger, lean into praise. In place of casting cynical glances from the sidelines, leap into a life of unabashed praise of God almighty.

Imagine with me the early Christian community as described in Acts. The people of God shared everything in common and lived continually praising God. No want, no need, no shame or sorrow! Everything given over to God's love as an act of praise for what God has done for us.

Yes, yes, some will say it's not realistic. Others will raise an eyebrow and bid us come to live in the real world. Still a few more will recommend therapy, but as for me and my house, we will praise the Lord!

Psalm 66:1-12

I use this psalm often when inviting people to join the church choir. The invitation comes and is frequently rebuffed with the comment that the person can't sing or can't even hold a tune. To this I respond readily, saying, "Scripture doesn't say we have to sing in perfect pitch. It says we have to make a 'joyful noise!' "

Indeed, joy seldom reflects the careful professional sounds of a large concert choir or orchestra. Joy is actually a little rowdy. It prances around like David dancing before God. It jumps, yells, and squeals in delight. Joy releases wonderful energy in unpredictable and chaotic ways. Joy defies our attempts to control and organize. Joy simply erupts.

This, of course, can cause problems in some church communities that prize order, discipline, and method. When God gets hold of someone's heart, such veneer is quickly peeled away in the wake of God's uncontainable love. Then our committees and strategy groups are left holding the organizational bag with nothing but copies of last month's minutes to contemplate.

Yet, balance is required. In my own church setting, my creativity and ability to try new ministries is made possible by the incredible organizational skills of the treasurer, who sees to it that the resources and tools necessary for ministry are available. This pastor's tendency to want to dance for joy is made possible by the discipline, focus, and hard work of another coworker in the Christian community. We are a team, mutually supporting one another, and mutually committed to God's kingdom.

Yes, it is about balance. Alongside David's joyful dance before God comes the dance of balance. This dance is the dance of James, who writes powerfully about the balance between faith and works. You simply cannot have one without the other. An important part of our faith journey certainly calls us to joyful abandon in the warm folds of God's love. We are, however, also called to discipline, rigor, and excellence. Without these, our joy can quickly disintegrate into frenzied running around, which quickly tires us and those around us.

Let's make that joyful noise to the Lord! Let's sing and prance and whirl about as we drink in the incredible and wonderful Spirit of the almighty God! While we dance, let's remember the balance that makes this dance possible. Let's live together into that balance, into that wonder that is born in Christian community.

Psalm 66:8-20

What does praise sound like? Is it a well-rehearsed choir uttering the sublime tones of the Rutter *Requiem*? Is it a gospel band pounding out funky rhythms and old growly tunes? Is it a church full of people with hands raised as they sing an old familiar hymn? Is it a children's choir, all beautiful and disarmingly out of key? Of course, it's all of this and more.

Praise is more than music and liturgy. Praise is response. It is an answer to what the holy has done in our lives. Praise is a way of saying thanks. It is the process of giving back to God some sort of gift that acknowledges God's holiness. If one stops to think about it, the whole of our lives really ought to be one continuous act of praise.

When we rise in the morning and see the magnificent work that is the human body, we should give praise. When we come down the stairs to make breakfast, we give praise that there is food and that we had shelter in the night. As we leave the house to go to the office or wherever it is we go, there is thanksgiving for good and meaningful work.

Even the way we engage others is a way of giving praise. Kindness offered to others is a way of saying thanks to God. Standing up for those who are oppressed is a way of thanking God for liberating us from our oppression. Taking the bold steps to become peacemakers makes it clear that we are thankful that God came among us as the Prince of Peace.

Praise is more than sound. It is more than words and prayer. Praise directed to the Lord our God is a life that has been changed by God's saving power. How might our lives be channeled to become a living voice of praise? How might the work of our congregations be focused to become vibrant centers of praise and justice?

How indeed might we all transform our lives into a stream of praise that brings not only honor to God, but healing and hope to God's creation?

Psalm 67

There is a popular bumper sticker that most everyone has seen of late. Usually it is printed on the background of red, white, and blue. The words boldly say, "God Bless America!" These sentiments echo the opening verses of this psalm. "May God be gracious to us and bless us and make his face to shine upon us." There is, however, one significant variation.

On the various placards and bumper stickers papering communities across the nation these days, the phrase comes not as a humble prayer request, but more like a demand. And so it is phrased: "God Bless America!" The contrast with this psalm is stark. The psalmist approaches with humility and praise, acknowledging God's sovereignty over all the nations. The psalmist acknowledges blessings already received and asks for God's guidance in the future. And once again, the prayer is bookmarked with unabashed praise for the one who gives the blessing.

For those sporting the quasi-religious patriotic bumper sticker, a few things might be noted. First, God has already blessed America in floods of abundance. God has blessed America with wealth and prosperity. God has blessed America with abundant natural resources and an incredible diversity of talent and spirit in its population. And God has blessed America with greater power than any other nation has ever known. Yes. God has blessed America. Certainly, we can pray for these blessings to continue. But first it might be wise to humbly acknowledge the manifold blessings that have been showered upon this nation.

Having noted blessings received, it might also behoove the faithful to take stock of how it is America has responded to the many blessings God has showered upon the nation. Having been blessed, in what ways is the nation a blessing to other nations? Having been blessed, how do the people then respond with justice and equity for all God's people?

The sin of nations throughout history has always been their tendency toward arrogance and the presumption of power, even over God himself. This psalm calls, not only the American nation, but all nations to a much needed reality check. It is, finally, God who's in charge. May God continue to bless the nation, and may its inhabitants remember that the God of blessing is also the God of guidance and judgment. May the prayer of words extend also to a silent prayer of hearing.

Psalm 68:1-10, 32-35

What are the attributes of God? Sitting in the midst of fifteen or twenty children each Sunday, the pastor asks these questions, "What is God like? How would you describe God?" One child's hand shoots up and he squeals out, "God is huge!" True. God is huge. So huge, in fact, that mere human capacity cannot comprehend even a portion of the reality of God. Another repeats the nearly vapid Sunday school aphorism that "God is love!" Also true. But the mining of 1 John is a mighty task not likely to be accomplished during the children's sermon. The pastor's own son looks slyly as his hand moves upward. "God," he says, "has a big, fat behind!"

After the waves of laughter coming from across the church begin to subside, and the pastor sets aside thoughts of revenge regarding his son, it begins to dawn on him that this is a nearly pointless exercise. Our nearly endless attempts to quantify and categorize God are about as laughable as the young boy's comment about God's posterior. There is no way to get a handle on the awesome reality of the divine. There is no possible arrangement of verbiage that can describe it.

But this much we can harvest from scripture. This much we can glean from 5,000 years of Judeo-Christian heritage. This much is clear. God is about justice. God is, as this psalm points out to us, "a father to orphans and protector of widows." God houses the homeless and leads the prisoners out of their cells into prosperity, and God sets the bar for "his" people, calling them to be the agents of this justice.

Across the landscape of our sacred texts this theme is steady. It soars above our private religiosity and mocks us as century after century we continue in our comical efforts to place the holy in a box that we can both define and therefore control. It is all rather pointless.

The bottom line, as far as the God of Israel is concerned, is justice. Eugene Peterson's "Message" paraphrases Amos 5:24 and pulls out the essence of it. "Do you know what I want? I want justice — oceans of it. I want fairness — rivers of it. That's what I want. That's all I want."

This psalm grasps this fundamental nature of God and chooses to celebrate it. It is a celebration that might well suit us today.

Psalm 71:1-6

Most people, at one time or another, have had the regrettable experience of needing refuge. Untold millions around this war-ripped world are literally refugees, whose lives are shattered as they are uprooted and left bereft of home, family, and any visible means of sustenance. Countless women around the world suffer from the brutality of abuse by their male partners and are in need of refuge. Each day the numbers of homeless poor on the streets of America grows and grows. They, too, need refuge.

The great likelihood is that most of the people reading these words will not require refuge in the way that those described above require it. Most will be able to understand the need. If not literally because of war or physical conflict, many have experienced a need for refuge within the context of human relationships. It could be conflict at work or within the family. It might be strife in the neighborhood or within the church congregation. A job can be lost, a loved one can pass away, calamity can strike in the form of a crippling disease — the list is endless. No matter how or where it occurs, most people know what it feels like to need a refuge in times of struggle. Most people know what it feels like to be in need of rescue.

The psalm under consideration here offers God as rescuer and refuge. This, of course, is a good thing. The hope is that people of faith everywhere would be able to embrace God as a "rock of refuge," in times of need. Moreover, the persistent hope would be that God would not be the rescuer of last resort. In other words, it would be a wonderful thing if God would be among the first resources reached for when trouble raises its head.

It's a good bet, though, that that is not usually the case. When strife or trouble comes home to roost, most folks run through the gamut of other available options before turning in desperation to God. Friends, family, lawyers, bosses, cops, and even preachers are more likely to be sought out before God is turned to as a rescuer.

The question begs asking. Why is that? Is it that faith is not strong enough? Is it that trust — or belief fails? Perhaps so. But it is more likely that God becomes the rescuer of last resort because there is no habit, no discipline, no practice of turning to God when times are pretty good. Could it be that the starting place for such holy refuge is as simple as the discipline of daily prayer? Is it feasible that a life that is practiced in turning to God in praise and celebration will more readily reach for that same God when the cause for celebration evaporates and trouble takes its place?

What if, as this psalmist indicates, God was the source of hope and help since the earliest days of childhood? Perhaps then, the consolation and refuge of the holy might well be present even as trouble knocks at the door. Maybe then the resources to deal with what life brings might all be a little easier to locate.

Psalm 71:1-6

Martin Luther wrote it. Many have sung it lustily on Sunday morning. "A mighty fortress is our God, a bulwark never failing!" Conjuring up God in this militaristic fashion gives some people pause. They see a fort bristling with weaponry and with armed soldiers at the ready. But this is not a fort in the sense that we may wish to use it for attack. It is a fort in the sense of a place of safety. "A rock of refuge."

It is a powerful thing indeed to conjure up images of a God who is a location of safety, a sanctuary for body and spirit. And for many this vision of God is operative. Perhaps it wouldn't hurt to take this understanding of the holy and see if it might go a little further. What would happen if the idea of refuge, of safety, of sanctuary was applied to the communities that are founded and built to worship and honor this God?

What if our local church communities were a "rock of refuge"? What if every church community committed itself to a Trinitarian concept of sanctuary?

This three-part formula would first include the church as sanctuary for the spirit. In this sense, our communities would be a safe place for people to become spiritually vulnerable so that they might stretch and grow into discipleship. The second sense of sanctuary would involve church as sanctuary for the heart. In this portion of our formula, people would be safe from criticism and ridicule; safe from wagging tongues and angry spirits. The last piece of this new Holy Trinity would be the notion of church as a sanctuary for the body. This means that the church pledges to keep people physically safe: no physical harm or abuse of any kind.

Such a fortress would be novel in society. There aren't very many places where people are safe in spirit, safe in their hearts, and physically safe all at the same time. Perhaps a beginning could be had in local churches. A covenant of sanctuary could be designed that would commit everyone in the church community to conduct themselves in a manner that would keep everyone safe.

Then, not only could we view our God as a safe haven, a rock, and a refuge, we could also create such safety within the folds of the communities that God has called us to build together.

Psalm 72:1-7, 10-14

This psalm hits the reader with laser-like precision. Only the most delusional or those awash in denial could miss the point here. Our faith is not one that can be spiritualized to the point of irrelevancy. Our faith has both calling and consequence here and now in the midst of the world's turmoil and craziness. More than that, our faith is bold enough to call the powers of the moment to account. It is a call that has not diminished over time.

"Give the king *your* justice, O God." These words, and those that follow, make it clear that the "principalities and powers" (Colossians 2:15) subscribe to a different operating definition of justice than does God. So it is that the call comes to grant the king God's justice. The tone is oppositional, and it is perhaps worth updating.

Grant the president *your* justice, O God. Not the justice of disappearing civil rights; not the justice of Guantanamo or Abu Ghraib, but your justice! If we take our faith seriously, what are we to do with sentiments such as this? There can be no denying that some "kings" have what one radio commentator called a "complex and adversarial relationship with the truth." Nor can it be denied that the nation is bogged down in an immoral and unjust war that is devastating to God's children in Baghdad and Boston — in Tikrit and Taos.

There's no question about it. This psalm is a summons to the faithful. It is a wake-up call to those who claim a faith in the God of Israel, the God who comes most powerfully to us in Jesus of Nazareth. This God desires justice and fair treatment to the poor and places the responsibility for this in the hands of the faithful. This God, in fact, would rather we not waste our time in church if our worship does not lead us to acting for justice and for peace (Isaiah 58:2-11; Amos 5:21 ff) in the world.

In a time when churches around the nation wrestle with mission and direction, these words need to be heard. In a day when the church is an object of ridicule because of its hypocrisy, these words need to be lived. And, in a day when oppression and violence are "standard operating procedure," our God calls us as never before to take a stand, to speak and act, not for the justice of the king, but for God's justice, in our communities, in our nation, and in our world.

Psalm 72:1-7, 10-14

What a prayer is uttered here! "Give the king *your* justice, O Lord." Of course, inflection is impossible to trace in any meaningful way and belongs to this writer only. Yet, the emphasis on the word, "your," is hard to resist. It is a bold, oppositional voice, indicating that they've had enough of the king's justice ... more than enough. The king does not look after the welfare of the poor. The king does not render righteous judgments. The king — in fact — has become the oppressor!

The king's descendents in power are no different. Enough, already. Give the king *God's* justice!

With eyes closed, the thought of such a thing overwhelms and brings tears to the eyes. Imagine a king or any contemporary variation thereof, actually wielding God's justice. In a world like this, it is almost beyond the scope of dreams. There would be prosperity for all the people, not just some. There would be care for the most vulnerable and the poor ... "those who have no helper." The poor would be defended, the oppressor crushed, and thanks be to God! Peace would abound.

This psalm resists, even denies the charge of utopianism or wide-eyed idealism. What is God's justice if it is not within reach? What is God's justice if the king is not, in fact, called to enact it? If such accusations are true, we are left only with a doe-eyed poem, melting saccharine and untrue on the tongue. Is this psalm merely a pastiche of empty wishes mouthed by fanciful dreamers?

The answer must be, "No," and again it must be said.

What a prayer is uttered here. Someone's father once said, "Be careful what you pray for, you just might get it." This psalm, it seems, invites just such prayers. So let's pray this psalm in the hope that we might just get it. Here. Now. Let us pray. "Give the king *your* justice, O Lord!" Having prayed it once, pray it again and again. Praying this psalm might lead us out of the smog-filled valleys of disempowerment. Praying this psalm might jolt us into new visions of faithfulness. Praying this psalm might awaken in us a passion for God's justice, not merely on some dusty biblical shelf, but in the world where Christ calls us into ministry and service.

So the invitation to prayer comes unsubtly upon us. The call to live into such a prayer echoes in our hearts. What would it take to pray this psalm into being? Perhaps the very things with which we are charged. Idealism? Guilty. Utopian vision? Guilty again. And there is more to march with these twins. Persistence, courage, boldness, and joy rise also to take a stand.

Then let us pray this psalm together. And let us know what a prayer is uttered here.

Psalm 72:1-7, 10-14

This psalm takes aim, not only at a once and long ago world, but also places the contemporary scene squarely in its sites. Though we have, in spite of appearances, given up kings and hereditary rights, the words come addressed to us. "Give the king your justice, O God...." The opening plea of this psalm makes it clear that there is a difference between God's justice, and that which passes for the same in the courts of royalty. And just in case we were wondering, the psalmist steps into the rarified air of clarity.

The people are to be judged with righteousness. As it is in today's justice system, "righteousness" comes usually to those who can afford a good attorney. Huge corporations with limitless resources are granted the legal rights of individual people, thereby depriving individual people of their rights. Equity and fairness are but a fleeting memory.

And the poor? They are left today to lives wrecked on the rhetorical shoals of "personal responsibility," and "globalization." Honorable employment that enables a person to support a family has evaporated into the midst of ever greater profits for corporations. More than 20% of the American population goes without health care, and the once-legendary middle class has shrunk as the rich grow richer and the poor grow poorer.

Yes, yes, the complaints come quickly. Don't bring your politics to church. Don't blame me. Let me worship God without all this social stuff, okay? Well, if we pay attention to scripture, it's not okay. This psalm is really just the tip of the biblical iceberg when it comes to a Christian voice for justice. People rooted in the Judeo-Christian heritage cannot escape it. We worship a God who demands a modicum of justice among the people. If this psalm isn't quite enough to tip the scales of the heart, check out Isaiah or Amos or Micah. Read chapters 5 through 7 in the gospel of Matthew, and don't forget the fourth chapter of Luke where Jesus stands up in the temple and announces himself.

Let's be clear. This isn't a call to take the ideology *du'jour* and pretend that it's God's will. Too often, Pharisees of all stripes try to stretch holy scripture over ideological agendas, pretending in a show of self-righteous zeal, that they are the arbiters of God's holy way. It's time, though, to stop playing around with God. It's time to stop manipulating the holy word to our own ends.

The call comes to enter into scripture, having dropped all of our agendas and pretenses. The shove of God's grace is at our back, pushing us to truly hear the word. "Give the king *your* justice, O God."

Psalm 72:1-7, 18-19

A wise teacher once pointed out that much of scripture is said in dialogue. It is a confusing point, at first. Certainly narrative and conversations between biblical figures are communicated throughout our Bible, but scripture itself as dialogue? How so? Well, think of it this way.

In Psalm 23, when the writer declares that the "Lord is my shepherd" (Psalm 23:1), this is not just a passing fancy. It is an announcement that a choice has been made. The Lord God of Israel is *my* shepherd, the implication being that there is a choice. And of course, we know that this is true. We can choose among gods as we see fit. The choice is between God our creator and redeemer, or as Paul indicates the God of our "belly" (Philippians 3:19). In the Lord's Prayer when the people pray, "thy will be done" (Matthew 6:10), it is a prayer for God's will, as opposed the will of others.

This sense of dialogical opposition is important in hearing holy scripture, and it is present as well in this psalm. The writer begins with the plea, "Give the king *your* justice, O God." Clearly there are other ideas about justice in play here. The writer is calling for God's justice and no other. And just in case the reader is unclear about this, the writer is happy to provide details.

God's justice gives fairness to the poor. It offers prosperity to the people and defends the needy, even going so far as to "crush their oppressor." This is God's justice. Justice that does not achieve this is not the justice of God. The king's justice, it would seem, does not come up to God's standards. So the call comes. The prayer is issued. Give the king your justice, O God. "Let justice roll down like waters, and righteousness like an everflowing stream" (Amos 5:24). Let this be "a day acceptable to the Lord!" (Isaiah 58:5).

So where, the question must come, is God's justice present today? Which "king" needs to discover the power and wonder of God's justice? Which ruler should be lifted up in prayer as the call comes for God's justice to reign down among the people? This is a question worth asking in prayer and dialogue, in discernment and community. It is a call that comes — not from political agenda or ideological stance — but rather from the holy word itself. Hear the prayerful plea echo down the centuries. "Give the king *your* justice, O God!"

Psalm 77:1-2, 11-20

It's one thing to talk the talk. Everyone knows people who are good at rhetoric. From coworkers to politicians to preachers and back again most people have heard so much talk that few are listening anymore. Indeed, the cultural landscape in which so many people are planted is one cacophonous wall of noise. Nothing but talk.

It's another thing altogether if you are able to also walk the walk. The words that come out of the mouth find depth and meaning when they are enfleshed in action. No one would read the sermons of Reverend Martin Luther King Jr. if he had not walked the walk. Dietrich Bonhoeffer's great theological works would likely have sunk far below the radar had this hero not stood firm against Nazi oppression. Think of the great heroes whose words and deeds have the decency to cohere into a unified, authentic life. Sojourner Truth, Dorothy Day, Daniel and Phillip Berrigan come instantly to mind. Thanks be to God, there are far more than these few mentioned here.

It is this sense of authenticity, of integrity, that pours from the words of this psalm. Here is a God who walks the talk. And if just saying so isn't enough, the psalmist is quite ready to enumerate the mighty deeds of the holy one!

Unlike other gods who stumble and fall, the holy God of Israel is a God who delivers. From Jacob and Joseph to the split of the Red Sea waters, this God comes through in the clinch. And for those who look through this window from a Christian lens, the story just keeps getting better.

In Christ, God keeps the prophets' promise and sends us the reconciliation of the cross. In Christ, a new covenant is forged and a new people born. And now, two millennia down the road the questions come. Are the people who follow this Messiah a people whose walk matches their talk? Are these people authentic and

106

ripe with integrity? Are these people anywhere near as faithful as the God who delivered them from sin and death?

These are questions worth asking and a conundrum worthy of confessional prayer. Are we a people who walk the talk of faith? Do we practice forgiveness? Do we offer grace? Do we accept injury rather than inflict it? Do we refrain from judgment?

Yes. This is a God worthy of praise. This is a mighty and holy God, a God who talks the talk in the living Word and walks the walk in that self-same utterance.

Psalm 78:1-4, 12-16

What are the stories we pass on to our children? Every family has them. My own father concocted an elaborate set of stories based on the adventures of an elf who lived in the forest around my childhood home. This elf had all kinds of adventures with various animals, with each story a moral that somehow fit into the particular childhood struggle occurring. I always marveled at how this elf led a life so parallel to my own.

Aside from family fairy tales and lore, we also pass on and tell other stories, don't we? Caught up, as we are, in our national mythos, we pass along stories of patriots and great leaders. We pass along tales of heroism and valor, and we pass on the narrative of our culture. One cultural narrative here in the United States would be the story line that says everyone has an equal shot at success. Another narrative would be that if we only work hard enough, success will be ours. True or not, these are the background stories for who we are as a nation.

How does this work for us as a people of faith? What stories about God do we hear and pass on to our children? More to the point, what stories do you pass on to your children about God? At dinner with family, at prayer time, on those long car journeys to Grandma's house, what is it that you tell your children about God?

The question is asked because it seems that the stories are told less these days. It's not that God's activity in the world has lessened. Indeed, look around and see everywhere the evidence of a loving and powerful God! Still, the stories don't seem to come to

— or from — us very much. Why, one is left to wonder, are we not telling our stories about God?

In an evermore secular climate some people, of course, are a little embarrassed to talk about God. Indeed, one church member who was putting on a benefit for a noble cause and was using the church sanctuary recently came and asked the pastor if he could cover up the cross and Christian symbols because he was afraid they might offend someone. Thankfully, the pastor politely declined to have the cross covered.

We also decline to tell the stories of God because we have so nicely compartmentalized our faith. Church or Christianity is what we do one morning a week and perhaps one evening for a committee or Bible study. It is seldom something that dominates our whole being. No, such extremism is for zealots.

So the question remains, not to be answered here, but by our daily living. How do the stories of God's mighty acts in history get told? Who tells them? Who is there to hear? Perhaps the call comes today for us to begin to share our stories with our children, our friends, with anyone who will listen.

Psalm 78:1-7

What are the things we teach our children? Anyone who is a parent would likely confess that they have taught the following things to their children: Don't talk to strangers; look both ways before crossing; don't do drugs or alcohol; and keep your room clean. Certainly this isn't an exhaustive list, but the point becomes clear. There are things that children need to be taught. Essentially, these things relate to survival. All good moms and dads want their kids to be okay. It's just that basic. As the psalmist relates, there are things we don't hide from our children.

However, it's doubtful that the psalmist was referring to inappropriate strangers or traffic lights. No, the "dark sayings of old" that get passed on from generation to generation have to do with the accumulated experiences of God. Yes, those experiences are sometimes "dark." From the floods of Noah to the Babylonian exile to the sufferings of our Lord, there are dark things that we dare not hide from our children. They do not stop at the pages of our Bible.

The father who reveals how God accompanied him through a brutal wartime experience is the father who relates a "dark saying of old." A mother who shares her own life struggles and how God was present in them also shares a "dark saying of old." The pastor who opens up and shares his or her own doubts and struggles with God shares "dark sayings of old." The story of a people of faith is, or ought to be, an accumulating volume of the felt experiences of God.

Unfortunately the stories are too often kept light and fun and within the confines of scripture. Picture, if you will, the light-filled paintings of Jesus with the little children on his lap. Pleasant and welcoming, to be sure, but such one-sided representations keep Emmanuel (God with us) too far from us. Yes, every parent should read and teach scripture to their children, but they should read it all. They should witness daily to God's present power in their lives. In this way children will learn to seek God's power in their own life experiences.

To the tried and true list of dos and don'ts it is important to add the "dark sayings of old" that come from the depths of our own souls as we struggle, wrestle, and walk through life with a wonderful and incredibly present God.

Psalm 79:1-9

Asking for forgiveness is not usually the first order of business for someone, even if they are obviously in the wrong. In order to ask for forgiveness, one has to first admit to having done wrong. And that, for most people, can be a difficult journey. In our faith tradition, it's called confession.

In the Protestant community, confession has lost much of its power. In some churches there is still a prayer of confession in the liturgy, but there is not much of an emphasis on a self-conscious, intentional effort to be open with God about our various missteps and misdeeds. The tendency is for many of us to simply move along through life's routines living in varying stages of denial about the things in our life that we have done, or left undone.

It takes a consequence to make us come clean. Often, the consequence has to do with getting caught in the act. A marital infidelity will often continue until it is discovered. Then, in the wake of disclosure and its ramifications, confession will come. The young child succumbing to the temptation to steal candy from the neighborhood store will often keep at it until he or she is caught. Then comes the confession and the plea for forgiveness.

There are times, of course, when forgiveness is not immediately forthcoming. This psalm emerges from the depths of consequences for grievous misdeeds. In the desolation of destruction and upheaval a whole people cry out to God for forgiveness. "How long, O Lord? Will you be angry forever?" It's like the child caught stealing money from the loose change jar. Reprimanded and punished, the child comes and seeks reconciliation. "Mommy, do you still love me?"

So the question comes: Where, in the lives we lead, do we need to ask for forgiveness? Where is it that our actions, or our inaction is something that has caused hurt or harm? Sometimes, the sin we commit is one of mute participation in a sin that the larger community is committing. How guilty, for example, was the average German for the sins of the Nazi regime? How guilty are we for the sins of our community? Are we responsible? Are we to be held accountable? Will we keep it up until, like the writer of this psalm, we grovel in the consequences of our sin and seek forgiveness from the depths of pain? Or is it possible — is it conceivable — that a person or a community can stop and take a good look in the mirror? And having looked, can we own up to the reality of our wrongdoing? If so, it just might avoid a world of hurt and pain.

Psalm 80:1-2, 8-19

There is a deep yearning here. A longing for a time now past. It seems that memory always burnishes the finish of bygone days. Listen closely to any gathering of older folk recalling the good old days. If honesty were to prevail, they probably weren't quite as good as recollection claims. But still, fortunes do decline. Armies invade. Economies stumble. Crops fail, and loved ones perish. In other words, even with an inclination to put a spin on the past, there are times when people ache for a restoration of good fortune.

History, of course, teaches that people and civilization move in cycles and long arcs of rise and decline. There is the movement and shove of cultures, the shift and jumble of intermingling traditions. Here lies something different. Here is desolation in the extreme. Here is a people who feel spurned by their God.

So the cry goes up. "Save us!"

In the wake of contemporary culture, the question arises. From what do twenty-first-century Americans need saving? If today's church community came together to cry out for restoration, what is it that would be restored? What kind of psalm would be sung to God if we were to fall on our knees and ask for God's help? Would the cry come to restore old "mainline denominations"? Would the old men and women gather in the church kitchen to recollect Norman Rockwell scenes of once and long ago? How would the people pray? What words, what yearning or longing would pass from their lips?

Perhaps it is longing itself that calls for restoration. Could it be that some ancient sense of yearning for God's intimate presence has evaporated in the wake of modern culture? Is it possible that the militant march of individualism has snatched holy intimacy away and replaced it with an incessant and wearying search for the self? Is there a chance that the self is somehow diminished or fractionalized by this vacuum where holy yearning once lived?

If there is a psalm of restoration to be written today, this could well be it. A fervent prayer for a reconnection to the holy is something that might well be considered. It might go something like this: Restore us, holy one, to relationship with you! Save us, Lord, from our empty search for a self that doesn't really exist apart from you. Bring us, we pray, into the fold of your embrace. Crack open our hearts and awaken our sense of longing, of yearning, our childlike sense of wonder at your magnificence. Restore us, O God, and come live in our hearts again. Amen.

Psalm 80:1-7, 17-19

My computer has a nice little feature. It's called "system restore." If, in my electronic ineptitude, I make a mistake, I can go to "system restore," and the computer will automatically restore my files to a point prior to my hapless fumble. Nice feature. It's clean — easy — and in a matter of moments, I am back to work on whatever project is before me.

System restore. Would that the people of Israel had such a feature in their life as a nation. Would that we had such a feature in our own life as individuals and community. Think about it. We mess up, and all we do is hit "system restore." Magically our lives return to a point before the mishap. No harm, no foul. Right?

Unfortunately, there are mistakes that strain even the ability of contemporary electronics engineers. A can of soda spilled on the keyboard by an overeager thirteen-year-old moves past a simple "system restore." A cruel infidelity in a marriage steps over the line of "oops." A people lured away from God to idolatrous and violent ways is somehow not fixed by the push of a button.

It is at this point that all pretense must be dropped. All feints and fancies that paint the air with excuses need to be halted. This is a time for blunt honesty. Any plea offered here must come from a "contrite heart" (Isaiah 57:14); a heart humbled by the acute awareness of complicity and culpability. The plea to be entered here can be no quick fix. It is no painless return to the status quo.

Restoration in this context looks rather more like transformation than return. With hurt and destruction, this deep thing simply cannot be the same again. Perhaps, herein lies the hidden beauty of our wounded nature. A "broken and contrite heart" (Psalm 51:17) can return to God in new and powerful ways. A relationship restored in the power and wonder of confession and forgiveness can go deeper and further than previously imagined. A people who embrace the forgiveness of their God can reach to new heights of faith and power.

"Restore us, O God," becomes a prayer for the ages; a plea for all who experience separation from the holy. Who, upon reading this psalm, can deny their brokenness? Who can gaze upon this ancient text and not feel the words arc back toward the heart like a boomerang of the spirit? This is a prayer for every mouth. From bishop to pastor to layperson and back again, it is a call forward. It pulls us together into a future of right relationship with one another and with God.

And so with open and honest hearts we pray with one voice, "Restore us, O God."

Psalm 80:1-7, 17-19

"It's time." These two words charged through the boy's consciousness like an electric shock. After all the practicing, all the hard work, all the waiting, it was finally time for his recital to begin. It was the moment that his gifts, graces, and discipline all strained to share. It was a conspiracy of grace. He stepped fearfully onto the stage, walked to his chair, and sat down. The maestro nodded. It was, finally, time. He put bow to string and began to play. And a hushed audience drank in the sounds of his brilliance.

Preparing and waiting are perhaps two of the hardest things we humans undertake. At least, they are difficult for us. First of all, we are lazy. We don't much like work, so preparation usually falls somewhere behind housework and the keeping of dental appointments in our list of priorities. Secondly, we are impatient. Waiting is hard. It requires patience and focus, and that capricious thing called vision. Perhaps this is why prodigies are such a rarity. And yet, there are times that call for both. Our journey in this season to the Messiah is such a time.

In these verses from Psalm 80, the writer voices a call for restoration from the depths of waiting. It is an impatient voice. It is a voice of suffering, a face of grief and sorrow. It is a people who have had no choice but to wait. One waits, it seems, when one must, but voluntary waiting is best left to Buddhists or Jesuits. The rest of us prefer a more immediate gratification.

In this moment, however, and for this people, the waiting is voluntary. It is a discipline of Spirit, preparation of our will, and a choice of faith. And, if taken seriously, it is not easy.

So the question comes. How do we prepare for a Messiah? What steps must we take to be ready? And as we prepare, how do

113

we wait? What are the choices we make? Can we sense the waiting of a broken, vanquished people? Can we pursue the preparation required to receive a Savior? Can we let go and embrace this God who comes?

Questions like these are carved like fine sculptures and designed to fit into the coming weeks as we pray, prepare, and wait. Perhaps it is in the dialogue of asking and answering, of preparing and waiting that we move forward as God's people in this potent and powerful time.

Psalm 81:1, 10-16

In talking about God, the conversation usually is about how we feel about God. The discussion will center around our experience of God and around our particular beliefs in and about God. But seldom do we pause to consider the world, or us, from God's point of view. What must God think? What must God feel? What, one wry preacher asked, is going on in the cosmic cranium?

Of course, it is probably folly to try to assign a human response mechanism to the creator of the universe. How could a grain of sand perceive the beach, let alone the ocean? Folly or no, it is difficult to resist simply because a human response is all we have. How else could we imagine God, except through the eyes, heart, and imagination that God gave us?

This psalm makes a run at the process and uncovers a God who seems a tad disappointed. More than that, this God seems to feel a bit shunned as well (he) might! "O that my people would listen to me!" One could almost imagine a brokenhearted God, pining over beloved children who simply will not listen. What parent can't identify with this?

And then, there is a capricious sense to this God. *If they would listen to me, then I'd help them out. But no. Since they are not listening I shall "give them over to their stubborn hearts and abandon them to their own council."*

It's an interesting exercise. One wonders how it might play out in the contemporary world. Try for a moment to put yourself in God's shoes. Does God have shoes? Likely not, but work with the pastor here! How do you imagine God viewing the people who claim to follow God in the United States in the present year? Look at these people. What must God think? What do you imagine to be God's reaction to how we conduct our affairs as a nation? As a church? Take a moment and write your own psalm from God's point of view. Perhaps this would be a good exercise for an adult study group, or even for a young peoples' group.

After the psalms have been written, compare the different points of view that God has in the differing psalms. What do these perspectives tell us about ourselves? Our faith? Our sense of call as a people? Then come together as a group and pray your way through these points of view and the things they reveal. It can be fun, and it just might spur some new growth and movement of the Spirit!

Psalm 82

God is taking stock of the way the gods, and note the small "g" here, are handling things. "How long," they are asked, "will you judge unjustly and show partiality to the wicked?" Good question. In a nation where 40% of the people have no health care worth mentioning, and in a time when the promises of pensions can evaporate with the bang of a judge's gavel, it is a good question, indeed. Injustice spreads like an infectious disease as more and more prisons are built in the shadows of crumbling schools and declining quality of education. It is not a slick liberal voice, or some practiced politico who asks, but God almighty. How long? How long will the poor carry the rich upon their backs while they get weaker and the bloated wealthy get heavier. How long?

Perhaps it is a rhetorical question, because it is followed by a directive, which indicates that God's patience is growing thin. There is thunder in the holy utterance: "Give justice to the weak and the orphan!"

Walk down almost any street in the United States and the weak are there to be seen. Homeless people, bent over by the rigors of street living; sick, tired, dying. It doesn't take a vivid imagination to paint a picture of justice for these people. It is a canvas brushed over with images of decent homes, jobs, health care, and a sense that they, too, matter. But it doesn't end with merely the weak. God clearly stands here on the side of those whom these lesser gods use as fodder. And indeed, judgment is coming.

How does the clarity of holy words such as this hit good religious folk in this day and age? What is the response of decent pew sitters who hear the voice of God calling for justice for the weak? Is it time for another prayer? Did we just see the pastor signal the organist to slide into another chorus of "Nearer My God To Thee"? Is it time to step over another prostrate figure on the sidewalk on the way to worship?

No, the days of numb acquiescence to the status quo are at an end. God speaks to the people and demands justice for the weak and the poor. God sits at table with the well-fed, prosperous, over-entertained and asks, "How long?" How long will this suffering be allowed to continue? How long will good Christians rest in comfort while poor people suffer?

The psalmist could not have read it, but may well have enjoyed Jesus' parable of the sheep and the goats. "If you did not do it to the least of these ... you did not do it to me ..." (Matthew 25:31-46).

Psalm 84

So many things come down to perspectives or points of view, don't they? It begs the question about which eyes are reading a scripture such as this. "How lovely is thy dwelling place!" The sense of longing here suggests the viewpoint of one who knows what it's like not to have a dwelling place; someone who understands what it feels like to feel that lack of God's presence. It brings to mind that old saying, "You don't miss the water till the well runs dry...."

Such depth of appreciation and wonder really can come only from an appreciation born of knowledge. Someone who has always lived in comfort and privilege will find it difficult to comprehend the motivations and actions of someone who is poor and homeless. Someone who has never been around the shattered homes and

116

lives of a war-torn community can find it easy to ignore wars sponsored by their own government.

But it is only those who have been homeless and destitute who can truly appreciate a home when it comes. None can savor the glories of peace more than those who have been the victims of war.

It is that the beauty of this psalm emerges from someone who has known and understands the struggle to seek, engage, and embrace the holy. Once found, once discovered, it is beyond wonderful. Happy are those who live in God's house! Happy are those who find their strength in God! This happiness, this joy, is infectious. It is the wonder of one who, after a long journey, discovers that it wasn't the destination that was important after all. It was the journey that mattered.

This psalm invites pilgrims on that journey. It sings to the spirit of travelers and it encourages those who have no hope as can only be done by those who have known hopelessness. Isn't it true that pastoral care works best if the pastor has experienced the circumstances or situation that calls for his or her care? In this writer's case, it is certainly true. Having lost one's parents, it becomes an easier thing to walk with others when they lose theirs. In this deep sense, this is a pastoral psalm. Its singing reaches to those who may not be in God's house; those who may not know what it means to trust anyone, let alone God. It reaches with knowing hands.

Psalm 85

Cynicism is in vogue these days. Perhaps it has never gone out of style. It just seems that in many a church circle these days there is a cynical wind, which attempts to blow out the candles of hope. Someone will get an idea. The response will be, "We tried that thirty years ago and it didn't work. What makes you think you can succeed?" Someone will get excited. The snide observation is a put down in thin disguise. "Calm down, won't you? You make me tired." Someone will be found praying, and the cynic will whisper, "Do you really think anyone is listening?" Cynicism like this poisons the waters of hope and chokes the breath out of the body of Christ.

117

But faith overcomes cynicism. Holy Spirit optimism drowns out persistent negative energy. And the intentional naïveté that comes with trusting God will prevail over all odds.

Psalm 85 displays this kind of faith and spirit. It emanates this kind of naive trust. There is no doubt here. There is no quarter given to naysayers or strutting narcissists. Here there is only certainty. Beautiful, clear, wonderful.

God *will* speak peace to the people. There is no hedging of bets here. All our money's on God's voice, and we can hear it now. God's salvation *is* at hand! Steadfast love and faithfulness *will* meet! Righteousness and peace *will* kiss each other!

No hint of cynicism or doubt here! Here only the clear waters of trust and certainty run and gurgle like a spring-fed stream. It's probably best to remember, too, that the words of this psalm were not likely penned by someone who was living in a bed of roses. Such trust didn't come from a full belly or an easy life but from the trials of life that put our faith to the test. The call to renew faith and trust can be heard in this psalm. Such certainty and clarity are things of beauty, giving life and sustenance in a world of cynicism and doubt.

Make no mistake about it. Such certainty and clarity are not intended to woo the faithful from the need for critical thinking and sober judgment. The need for these will never wane. But in these days of "post-modern" thought, where the "de-construction" of all things is the rage, a little certainty won't hurt. A clarity just might help.

Psalm 85:1-2, 8-13

Hope is a concept that contemporary Christians do not engage with much competence. Awash as we are in this culture, we find ourselves having reduced hope to a vain and empty wish. In the morning we step outside and we *hope* it won't rain today. We *hope* that the boss will like us. If you're a pastor, you find yourself *hoping* that Sunday's attendance will be at least the same as last week. And please God, don't let it be less! For too many of us, the Christian notion of hope has drifted far from our home shores, leaving

118

us with the inadequate and mistaken notion of hope huckster'd by talking heads and mail-order catalogues.

But for a people of faith, hope must be something else.

For us, hope must articulate a certainty that we cannot back up with any forensic proof. This, of course, is sheer silliness to the society around us. How could anyone proclaim something that cannot be proven? It is, in the circles in which I travel, worth a giggle at least, and yet, we hear such certainty in the words of this psalmist.

It is not an empty wish that speaks with such force. God *will* speak peace to the people! Steadfast love and faithfulness *will* meet. Righteousness and peace will kiss. Faithfulness *will* spring up from the ground and righteousness *will* look down from the sky.

The psalm allows no flip-flopping or discussion. These things are going to take place. It is believed so thoroughly, so deeply, and so completely — without evidence — that we begin to live as though it were true.

In faith, in community, in witness, and yes, in hope, we become the fulfilling instrument of God's desires. We hear the voice of God calling us to be peacemakers, and rather than throw our hands up in impotence at the horrors that war is raining down on our world, we become peacemakers. Rather than following the shallow dictates of a selfish culture, we become God's witness to steadfast love and faithfulness. In our relationships, in our work, in our lives we become the integrity that God proclaims.

These words have power in the face of a disempowering world. They are words that call us to a radical trust in a God who comes. They are words that dare us to hope in new and life-giving ways. They are words that believe the promise of God and are willing to live into that promise.

Psalm 86:1-10, 16-17

Having someone hate you is a difficult thing to bear. Having someone hate you and then try to do something against you is even worse. The fear, the sense of powerlessness, and the insecurity one feels at a time like this is difficult to describe. The whole body fills with tension. It's difficult to focus or concentrate. Over and over again the mind wonders what was done to deserve this. In between that wondering comes the playing and replaying of scenarios about how things might have gone differently.

Being under attack like that consumes one's spirit and energy. It sucks the life right out of the soul. It's this sense of despair and sorrow that this psalm conveys. It's this feeling of being boxed in and without options that leads to the plaintive cry to God.

Those who haven't had an experience like this can count themselves among the blessed. But if it is happening, if someone is out to get you, the call rises from the belly and rockets to the ear of the holy. "Listen to me! I'm calling on you, God!"

If help doesn't seem to be forthcoming, the desperation grows to a manic mantra of attempted persuasion and even flattery. "There's no one like you, God. All the nations will come and bow before you. Bank on it! You're the greatest!"

Reading this psalm wrenches the heart. Down the centuries one can feel the pain and the anguish in these words. More powerful than that is the truth that these words are rooted in the firm and sure belief that indeed God is listening. Indeed, God will save. These are no vaporous utterings floating off into nothingness. These are not words given to an eternal silence. This prayer, like every prayer, is heard. This prayer is embraced by a God who is engaged and active in the panoply of history.

This pronouncement should be the end of it. The prayer is offered. The prayer is heard. But the cynic within sighs deeply and rolls imaginary eyes. "The prayer may be heard, but is it answered? Didn't prayers like this go up the chimneys of Dachau? Didn't prayers like this get lifted up in countless scenes of suffering across the globe? Where," the inner cynic asks, "is the answer to the prayer?"

This inner cynic is tough, and for him there are no easy answers. Perhaps that's why he's a cynic. Cynics like easy answers.

The persistence of faith insists on this: God is real. God created us. God loves us. Indeed, God is love itself (1 John 4:8). It all comes to the realization that God is not an old, white man with a

120

beard running the world as a puppet master manipulates his subject across a dusty stage.

No, it's a bit more complex than that. Between our freedom to do as we choose and God's ever-present grace, between our seemingly endless capacity to choose death over life (Deuteronomy 30:15-20), and God's truly endless capacity to love, in between all this comes the one moment we have to trust in God no matter what is happening. That moment is the one we are living right now. It is the ever-flowing present tense; the eternal now into which we give our trust. And trust, it must be said, is not a cynic's tool.

Psalm 89:1-4, 19-26

Today we live in a world where all our leaders are "deconstructed." Every frailty of every hero is laid out with devilish glee so that we might witness their feet of clay. One had issues with fidelity in marriage. Another may have copied parts of an academic paper. Still another had financial troubles. On it goes until the people dare not trust anyone for fear of trusting in one who might have a weakness. Worse still, those who may feel called to leadership hesitate because — God forbid — they, too, may have some skeleton in their closet. We even try it with Jesus himself! Novelists conjure up fictional marriages and forays into Jesus' alleged "lost years," and scholars obsess with what he really said.

No one is safe from the deconstructionist leer that leans close in and says, "No one could be that good!"

So it should be an easy thing for us to hoist this poem aloft and say it together. Do we not long for a leader who is "mighty" and "chosen from the people"? Wouldn't we love to look up to someone who was just and good? Someone who is caring and compassionate? Do we not all dream of a leader who cares more for the people than for ... well ... you fill in the blank.

But wait. This is the season of Advent. This deep longing *will* be filled. This hunger *will* be satisfied. This thirst *will* be quenched. We shall have a king who is one of us. We shall have a Savior who is mighty indeed. We shall receive a ruler who cannot be outwitted or brought low. We shall have Jesus Christ as our king!

121

There, now we can all open our gifts before sitting down to dinner. Right?

Well, yes. And no. With all due respect to the separation of church and state, we need to note here that choices are being made. We need to be attentive when we lay such titles at the feet of Jesus of Nazareth. Jesus is king? Jesus is Lord? If he indeed is to be our king, then we can have no other. Are we quite ready for that? If indeed our loyalty and allegiance are to go to this Lord, this coming messiah, then there are others who will think us disloyal ... even unpatriotic. Do we really want to go there?

Do we really want this Savior?

In this moment, let the prayer go forth that we might accept this king, this Messiah, this Savior who is to come. Let the prayer escape from our hearts and part our lips, that we might embrace this anointed one with all our hearts, all our minds, and all our spirits.

Psalm 89:20-37

What a beautiful thing is rendered here. A covenant made and kept. A promise uttered and maintained. God's faithfulness to the line of David is unalterable. Promises kept are powerful things, aren't they? It's been told to many a child by parents and caregivers that a person's word is their bond. Think about the people we trust the most in our lives. They are inevitably the ones who keep their word. The need to keep our promises is one of the things that literally makes life possible. The glue of culture, in fact, is the ability to trust that people will do what they say they will do.

The mechanic who says he will fix your car, the person who says they will pay you for services rendered, the employer who promises a pension plan and health insurance. We need to trust in promises such as these, or none of us are going to do very well. Indeed, it can be said, with little fear of contradiction, that the sense of faltering we feel in our culture today is linked in no small way to the dissolution of this concept.

It could be argued that we have, as a people, abandoned the notion of commitment. No longer must we do what we say we will do. From the vapid promises of politicians to marriage vows to workplace commitments and back again, we have fallen into the murky shadows of situational ethics. We have heard it before. "I meant it when I said it ... but ... well ... things have changed." The fact that a promise was made didn't change. The reality of a covenant made in marriage isn't changed because a man in mid-life turmoil seeks a younger woman to try to beat back the march of time.

This abandonment of commitment seeps into relationships where people refuse to make a "commitment." It even pervades the life of the church, where few people commit these days to leadership roles or things that mean they will have to follow through and be present.

A sociologist may well argue the point, but for people of faith this much remains. We exist as a people because of a promise made and kept. Consider the words of Jeremiah: "I will be their God, and they shall be my people" (Jeremiah 31:33). This covenant, or contract, followed up so marvelously by the new covenant in Christ, makes us who we are. It is promises made and kept that give us our very identity. So read this psalm with reverence. Absorb these words as a signpost and reminder that we are who we are because of promises made and kept.

Psalm 90:1-6, 13-17

It was Rene Descartes who said, "I think, therefore I am." While not wishing to enter the questionable theological ground of this statement, it is interesting to note that such ability to reason has plagued humanity for centuries. We are capable of discerning our place in the universe and at once are both awed and overwhelmed by it. It is with similar confusion that we approach the comprehension of the reality of God.

From our finite and limited point of view it is virtually impossible to imagine God. Yet this psalm attempts it with beauty, calling up images of eons before mountains were formed and even a nod to the formation of the earth itself. Mortality, dust, time, all of it enters into these few verses and spills forth with a sense of muted awe.

Even though the practice of pulling Christian images and thoughts from pre-Christian texts is frowned upon by scholars, there is a point to be made here.

It is this very inability to comprehend God that makes the incarnation in Jesus so very powerful. Even the beautiful language and poetry of this psalm does not give the heart a grasping place to touch the holy. But in Christ Jesus we have a God with handles. In his humanity, Jesus is accessible in unbelievably wonderful ways.

Jesus in the scriptures is seen as very human. One moment he is gentle, the next racked with frustration. Another time he rolls his eyes in vexation at his followers while yet another he pulls out a bullwhip and drives the money changers from the temple. This Jesus kneels in love to heal. This Jesus grows harsh as he condemns those who make a mockery of faith. This Jesus asks out loud if the cup can pass from him. This so very human reflection is someone that we all can relate to in deep and life-changing ways.

While the psalm blazes with beauty in its attempt to relate the wonder of God, this writer is thankful for the revelation that has come to us in Christ. Still, God is unsearchable, unfathomable, and unknowable. But now in Christ, he has come near.

Psalm 91:1-2, 9-16

This psalm represents a real struggle for most people. Simply put, the psalmist is positing that if you trust enough in God, no evil will befall you. At the risk of contradicting scripture, let it be said that even the most simple among us know this to be false. The world is full of good God-trusting people who have fallen victim to evil. From innocents who happen to be in the path of a bomb dropped from 20,000 feet to the millions around the world who succumb to the AIDS pandemic, the innocent do perish no matter how much they trust in God. Certainly, as Christians, we know what happened to Jesus who trusted God and went the distance to the cross.

No pastor worth his or her salt would ever let congregants believe that Christian faith amounts to an insurance policy against bad things happening. Yet here in this psalm, the faithful must contend with what was obviously a part of Jewish piety at the time that this was written.

Let it be said, instead, that the protection that the faithful receive from God is not safety from life's calamities. It is the security and sense of power that comes from the assurance that God accompanies the faithful through life's travails. Paul says it best in Romans.

> *What then are we to say about these things? If God is for us, who is against us? He who did not withhold his own Son, but gave him up for all of us, will he not with him also give us everything else? Who will bring any charge against God's elect? It is God who justifies. Who is to condemn? It is Christ Jesus, who died, yes, who was raised, who is at the right hand of God, who indeed intercedes for us. Who will separate us from the love of Christ? Will hardship, or distress, or persecution, or famine, or nakedness, or peril, or sword? As it is written, "For your sake we are being killed all day long; we are accounted as sheep to be slaughtered." No, in all these things we are more than conquerors through him who loved us. For I am convinced that neither death, nor life, nor angels, nor rulers, nor things present, nor things to come, nor powers, nor height, nor depth, nor anything else in all creation, will be able to separate us from the love of God in Christ Jesus our Lord.*
>
> — Romans 8:31-39

Indeed, our trust in God is not betrayed when trouble arrives. We are, instead, accompanied through these woes by a mighty Savior.

Psalm 91:1-6, 14-16

Go ahead. Take a coin from your pocket. Hold it up and look to see where it says, "In God We Trust." It is quite a statement. Trust itself is something when it is actually accomplished. Think, for example, about the number of people in your life who have your full, unqualified trust. If you're like most people, the number is not high. Trust is hard. It requires vulnerability, and no one likes feeling vulnerable. Yet, the path of faith is the process of becoming vulnerable, not to a person, but to God.

Christians are sticklers about believing. The question *du jour* for many folks has to do with whether or not someone believes in God or believes that Jesus is the Messiah. But the rubber really hits the road on the trust issue. In fact, in the New Testament, the Greek word that is translated often as "believe," is actually *pistus*, which means trust. Trusting someone means that you look to that person for security, for safety, for consistency, and for reliability. The *Peanuts* cartoon comes to mind, where good old Charlie Brown keeps trusting Lucy not to remove the football as he rushes up to kick it. Lucy, it turns out, is not trustworthy. But God? God is worthy of our trust.

It's worth considering the question of our trust in God. Do we trust God? If so, our life is going to look and feel a little different than those who choose not to trust God. Do we trust in God to provide? Do we locate our sense of security and safety in God? Do we lean into God's providence, even, or especially, when things are going badly? Or do we trust God merely when things are going our way? Actually, it's trusting in God when the chips are down that really counts. Someone once said that being a pacifist between wars was like being a vegetarian between meals. It is precisely when life's challenges confront us that our trust in God is most critical.

Trusting in one thing reflects a choice. It means that we choose not to trust other gods. Choosing the God of Israel as our God means that we do not place our trust, for example, in money. This is perhaps the thinking behind whoever decided to put the statement upon our money. We may spend money every day, but our trust is elsewhere. If we place our trust in God, and lean into God for our security, then we do not — indeed we cannot — trust in weapons of war to protect us. If we trust in God, then we need not worry about the vagaries of this world. See how the gospel of Matthew reflects the call of this psalm to trust in God. Read carefully Matthew 6:25-34.

"So do not worry about tomorrow, for tomorrow will bring worries of its own. Today's trouble is enough for today" (Matthew 6:34).

Perhaps Jesus reflected on this psalm? Perhaps with him, we can lean into this sacred trust. Perhaps in him we can walk together in faithfulness.

Psalm 95

In democratic culture, individualism reigns supreme. Each man and woman is trumpeted as master of his or her destiny and is free to pursue happiness as they deem fit. It is this kind of cultural assumption that lies behind the question that gets asked of every six-year-old, "What do you want to be when you grow up?" The answers that come are delightful, of course. Beaming parents field answers like, ballerina, firefighter, police officer, and a hundred other options. But the operative assumption in this ritual is that each of these six-year-old children has a better than even chance of becoming anything they desire.

Before the fall of the Soviet Union and the demise of its client states, a group of children in an elementary school in Dresden, Germany, were asked the same question, "What do you want to be when you grow up?" Instead of a response, there was a stony, mystified silence in the room. "What do I want to be? What's that got to do with anything?" As it turned out, such a question focusing on the fulfillment of individual desires or wants was so alien that it never even occurred to these children. The question these children were asked was not what they wanted, but instead what did their nation need? To devote one's life energy to pursuing a personal goal was thought in this culture to be selfish, even destructive.

These two poles of individual and communal orientation lead directly to the reading of this wonderful psalm. Here is a full-blown explosion of praise to the creator God! All stops are pulled out in favor of a glorious, passionate expression of praise. It doesn't even matter if the choir is on key. Just make a joyful noise! Give glory and honor to God! Enter God's presence with thanksgiving!

In short, the psalm is a powerful utterance that speaks the location of allegiance. Here there are no individual desires staked out with prayer requests. Neither are there calls to communal commitment, wondering what the collective needs most. No, instead the writer simply lays out an ultimate commitment to God.

So it is that a person of faith, whether growing up in middle-class USA or the worker's paradise of the German Democratic Republic would not be concerned with either individual or collective needs. Instead, the person of faith who shouts out God's praise and dances with a passion for the Lord asks quite another question altogether. Indeed it is formed more like a prayer than a question.

It's not what I want, God, nor is it what the state expects. But in all things, Lord, let me be led by you. Amen.

Psalm 96

"Say to the nations, 'The Lord is king!' "

Our religious vocabulary is full of such claims as this. On this night, especially, we look forward to the birth of the "Prince of Peace." Indeed, there are likely a few who have taken the time to sing or to listen to Handel's *Messiah* where we laud the "King of kings and Lord of lords!" In a culture where we attempt to draw boundaries between church and state, such claims can be confusing at best.

If God is king ... or to use modern parlance, president, then what do we do with the fellow occupying the office at 1600 Pennsylvania Avenue? After all, we hear in scripture that we cannot have two masters, for we will love one and hate the other (Matthew 6:24). What, one has to ask, are good Christians to do?

Some follow the impulse to "Christianize" the government. We are, after all, a "Christian nation." The fiction of this former statement notwithstanding, this is a route followed by a vocal minority. Another impulse might be to ignore the guy in the White

House and try to simply follow God's law — assuming we can find consensus on that.

Neither of these options seem satisfactory, even as we await the birth of the King of kings. Perhaps a modest suggestion is in order.

What if our language revealed to us a hierarchy of sorts? What if this Messiah, this Prince of Peace, this Emmanuel, is indeed our true leader? To this one we owe our final fealty. This, however, does not erase the need for a viable civil government that guarantees the rights of all and protects the most vulnerable among us. Even with Jesus Christ as Lord, we will still need roads, hospitals, schools, and a decent sanitation department.

The difficulty comes, however, when civil government asks or demands things of us that we know will not please God. Herein lies the call to conscience, the opportunity for prayer and debate, the need for open hearts and committed lives of prayer. And, as Martin Luther King Jr., Daniel Berrigan, Dorothy Day, and a host of others have done, it may come to a choice to prayerfully disobey the civil government in order to maintain obedience to God. Remember, it has ever been thus. Even Saint Paul was forced to write some of his letters from a jail cell.

So what say you? On this Christmas Eve, let the bells ring out! Let the celebration begin! For Christ our Lord is born! He is our sovereign Lord, who claims our final loyalty. As we gaze on the manger scene let us also gaze on the public square where together we meet the common need and advance the cause of the vulnerable among us.

Psalm 97

This is it. All bets are off tonight, because somewhere in a feeding trough at the back of an old stable, God decided to make an appearance. God has done a mighty thing and come among us ... as a helpless baby. God shows up all right. But can this be right? God as refugee?

Most of us would prefer this "psalm of enthronement," as scholars call it. We like this. It's time for a party. "Let the earth rejoice!"

129

And so we should. But, a refugee God? A God whose foundation for rule is "righteousness and justice"? Wow.

Maybe it's time to sit down and think this through.

The psalms, of course, cannot be stretched to do our twenty-first-century Christian bidding. Yet much of what we understand of lordship and praise, of the dominion of God comes from these incredible verses. Further, we do believe and trust that the God who is described in this psalm is the self same one who is soon to need a change of diapers in the hay. This creator God, enveloped in clouds and making the very earth to tremble, seems to be trying something new tonight.

Can we see it? Can we ourselves try to grasp what it means for the creator to come among us as a helpless infant? What does this say to us of power? What does this say to us of justice and right action? How are we to be different, now that the Lord of glory has made an entrance like this?

Let this birthing night ask these questions. Let this labor give birth to new understandings and brighter clarity. If God's enthronement can move from mountains melting and heavens proclaiming to a baby with tiny hands that grab around your fingers, can we not also imagine different lives for ourselves?

Could we perhaps open our eyes to the possibility that power lives, not in coercion, but in vulnerability? Might we examine the notion that justice and right action are not only the foundations for God's rule in this psalm, but also the foundation stones for our lives? If God can rule from such a foundation, imagine a church built on those same blocks! If God can come among us in this moment in weakness and vulnerability, can we not go forward in the same way, full of love? Full of hope? Full of new life?

Because God does come like this, we know that the answer to the foregoing questions must be "Yes." And it is this yes, this answer that moves us forward as God's people in a new time.

So Merry Christmas. Let each of us celebrate this day with that same loud "Yes," shouted with rejoicing and with joy.

Psalm 97

Christ is born! Amidst the piles of wrapping paper and gifts; across the tables of feasting and family there is the simple, passionate call to rejoice. "The Lord is King! Let the earth rejoice!" Who can deny it? Across Christendom we celebrate the coming of the Christ Child, a new birth, a new chance, a new beginning has come upon us, and all we need do is seize the moment. *Carpe diem!*

All this is well and good, and a Merry Christmas ought not to be impeded by a preacher's too-serious tone. Yet it needs to be said that there is a small item that slips by us in the psalmist's call to rejoice in the kingship of the Lord. Well, perhaps it's not small.

Living, as we do, in a republic that long ago gave up pretenses to royal families and kings, it is difficult for us to hear the full implications of the resounding statement that the "Lord is king!" And there is no better day to get clear about this than Christmas Day. When we shout with the psalmist that the "Lord is king," we've said a mouthful without realizing it. Then, as now, kings are kind of jealous of their power. They don't appreciate competition. If the Lord God is king, then whoever it is that sits on that golden throne is in for a rude shock. If we truly wanted to update this phrase so that a twenty-first-century American might truly understand it, we would say it like this. "Let's party because God is the president!"

It's a good bet that past, current, and future occupants of the White House might be a little uncomfortable with the idea that the power they wield really isn't their power at all. Of course, there is a place for kings and presidents. There's a role for governments and kingdoms. Building hospitals, roads, schools, and bettering the lot of the people is all within the realm of God's vision for human leadership and government.

Not within the power of kings or presidents is the taking of life. Not within the power of prime ministers or dictators is the destruction of God's creation. Not within the power of any government is the slaughter of innocent people of any nationality or race in indiscriminate warfare.

131

On Christmas Day as we open our hearts in joy to the coming of our Savior we, as Christians, are called to grow into the realization that our first allegiance is to God and to God alone. It's Christmas Day! For a moment at least, let us be prayerful. Let us be clear. Let us say, "Rejoice, for the Lord is king!"

Psalm 97

Bracketed by the language of praise, this psalm tackles an issue that does not much concern the church these days. For contemporary Christians in North America, idols are something out of teen fashion magazines or television shows where people embarrass themselves trying to gain the glitter of momentary fame. But for a biblical people, idolatry is — or should be — serious business.

Idolatry has to do with breaking covenant with God. It has to do with turning away from our sovereign creator God and giving our allegiance to other "gods." Idolatry, finally, has to do with our own infidelity to the one God of Israel, the God who comes to us in Jesus Christ. The worship of false gods or images is nothing new. From the golden calf (Exodus 32:4) to the Baal cults, to the Roman gods, and on into our history as a people of faith, we have wrestled with idols. The attraction, of course, is understandable. Idols can be seen, felt, and touched. Idols also tend to offer easy answers and quick solutions, and idols always lure us away from fidelity to the one God of Israel.

It's an easy thing to glance back through the lens of history and cast a judgmental eye on those who would worship statues or fertility gods or golden calves. But in reading this psalm through, the question arises. What are the idols to which Christian people succumb in these early years of the twenty-first century? Has the so-called post-modern age outgrown idolatry? Or has the contemporary community merely traded in the statues of old for new idols?

It can be said with little fear of contradiction that we contemporary folk do not sit in a place of privilege or freedom from guilt here. Idolatry continues in the church today, perhaps more so than in the past because no one wishes to address the topic. While it may not take the form of following after the cult of Baal, it does exist.

It might be a good exercise for a contemporary congregation to meditate upon idolatry and the forms it takes in today's churches. What are the idols? How do they lead us away from God? What are the consequences of contemporary idolatry? How might the church work its way back to fidelity to the covenant with God?

This, perhaps, is no easy task. But there are few that are more significant in terms of the future of God's church.

Psalm 98

Some people are gifted in music. They can sit down and play an instrument the first time they touch it. Others are not so blessed. For them, music comes with difficulty. Carrying a tune is hard, even if they have a bucket. But gifted or not, it seems that most of us share a love of the music we already know. Whether it's hymns or popular music, classical or country, we all relax into the strains of music we find familiar. Like a favorite chair or flannel shirt, we cling to the comfort of what we know.

At Christmastime, we see this in our love of the great, old carols. We delight in the sounds and warm each year to the memories that populate each note we sing.

Yet, on this day we hear the psalmist urging us to "sing a new song."

A new what? What's going on here? Is there something wrong with the old songs? Why on earth should a new song be sung — especially at this time of year? The resistance to learning and singing new songs is palpable. It can be felt in the cold winter air.

When it comes to Christmas and Easter, some of us don't like new songs much at all. New songs take energy to learn. New songs jolt us out of our comfort zone. New songs mean new words, new notes. They mean ... change.

But a new song is exactly what this day calls us to sing. Jesus Christ is born! God is doing a new thing, a mighty thing, and what could be more fitting than a new song? What could be more appropriate than singing new notes of praise, shouting new lyrics of love and fidelity? Can we do anything less than compose a new symphony of praise? Would we dare to do anything else but make a new and joyful noise to a God who comes to journey with us through these difficult days?

It's Christmas. The baby is born. The Messiah is come, and new possibilities hang in the air like incense in a cathedral. Should we? Could we? Dare we? Perhaps, for a moment, we might step out of our comfort and ease to welcome the one who is born into the cold. Maybe we might — just this once — set aside the familiar well-worn tunes to try a few verses of something new?

Try it. Make it up, even. Hum a few bars, and maybe everyone could join in the new song together. For indeed, this God child deserves a new song. Come, let's sing it together.

Psalm 98

Anyone who has made a long road trip with children singing "99 Bottles Of Beer On The Wall" can support the notion of "singing a new song." Children love the repetition of singing the same song over and over. Parents or youth group leaders who have been in this situation can identify with the need to sing a new song.

It's difficult to admit, but beyond the well-worn familiarity and comfort, songs do get old. They lose their punch and immediacy through time. We may like that old chestnut, but those who have come into life through a different set of experiences don't necessarily see how wonderful that old song is to some of us. Perhaps it is time to learn a new tune.

Yet how difficult that is for us. Across hundreds of different faith communities the so-called worship wars rage. Contemporary versus traditional, young versus old, modern versus old-fashioned, and on and on it goes. Sing a new song? That is just about as hard as switching from "trespasses" to "debts" in the Lord's Prayer.

It isn't that we don't have reason to sing. Look, after all, at what God has done for us! God has done "marvelous things." God has won the victory for us and vindicated us. God has remembered the people and loved them well. At some level we do know this. But still, that strange tune, and those new words?

One is led to wonder if our problem with singing the new song isn't about style or cultural differences, but rather about our heart-felt experience of God's vindicating and healing love. If we as a people truly experienced God as vindicator and steadfast lover, how could we not sing a new song? If we, for even a moment, opened our collective mind and hearts to the power and wonder of this God, singing and praising would simply erupt spontaneously.

As it is, we are caught up, not in new songs sung to God, but in arguing over which music *we* like best. To God, this sounds like "99 Bottles Of Beer On The Wall" when you're on bottle number 83. Let's be candid. Our old songs are great. Our familiar ways of experiencing God are wonderful. The bottom line, however, isn't what *we* like in terms of music or style or tone. It's not about us. It's about God. It's about bringing as many people as possible into contact with God's amazing love for us in Jesus Christ. Is it possible that our old songs hinder that process?

What would it take for us to stumble into a new experience of the holy? What steps would we take, what disciplines might we practice? How might we let go of what we like and spend a little effort learning that new song? It's easy, really. Just hum a few bars and let others follow along.

Psalm 98

Rolling the radio around the stations one morning during summer vacation, it became evident that there is not much of a taste for "new songs." From static to station and back again, the radio dial was alive with oldies stations. Hits from the '50s, '60s, '70s, '80s, and now even the '90s! Oldies. Each decade claims a niche of style, a series of songs that generations sing through adolescence and hopefully, into adulthood. These songs are reveled in, each one serving as a benchmark for a memory that improves in quality with the passage of time.

Oldies are, of course, fine. It's great fun to pull out those old 33 1/3 vinyl records and place them on the turntable. Even more fun is to watch the amazement on the faces of the young, who are all plugged in with MP3 files and other high tech means of listening.

They can scarcely believe that such antiquity still exists, let alone actually works!

But it is these young ones who are listening to a "new song." One wonders if they, too, will be cemented to their "oldies" as time marches on for them. Is it only the young who can sing a "new song"? Is each successive generation condemned to being hand-cuffed to the past? And if so, why is that?

This psalm calls us to sing a "new song" to the Lord. But how many congregations and parishes are stuck singing the oldies? How often have people intoned this phrase in one form or another? "We've always done it this way." Or, "We tried that once and it didn't work...." Yes, it's true. People tend to find memory's niche and build a nest therein. They decorate the walls of this nest with distortions and blurred vision of how things really were in those good old days.

Through it all, however, the call still comes to sing a "new song" to the Lord. One can't help but wonder what that might look like in today's cultural milieu. Is it bringing a "praise band" into worship? Perhaps. Is it celebrating ethnic diversity and trying to worship in different languages? Possibly. It could be these or a host of other new tunes taking the shape of worship, fellowship, mission, and witness. However the song goes, this new song, sung to the Lord, must also be sung to the community in which the church exists.

If the people in the community hear the song and turn off the radio, it doesn't do much good, does it? Yes. This new song must be sung to the Lord, but the Lord isn't the only one in the audience. The church today needs to reach out with this new song to welcome, to witness, and yes to evangelize a whole new generation who have yet to discover the wonder of this God who deserves our songs.

Psalm 99

One of the realities that inhibits our understanding of biblical language is the fact that we really don't have much to do with kings these days. Certainly, there is the celebrity-based fascination with the late Princess Diana, and the fevered click of the cameras around Britain's royal family, but truthfully, kings and queens don't have much to do with us today. They especially don't touch us as sources of power in our world.

Power comes from dictators, prime ministers, and presidents. It doesn't much flow from a king anymore. So to say "The Lord is king," evokes a yawn from most contemporary listeners. But, if the language of power were updated and we were to claim, "The Lord is our president!" it's guaranteed that more than a few people might turn to listen. As it turns out, there's someone living on Pennsylvania Avenue who is quite convinced that he is the president. If we claim that the Lord is president, then we have a bit of a conflict.

Jesus understood this clearly when he said, "[You] can't have two masters, for you will love the one and hate the other" (Matthew 6:24). This psalm also has a clear understanding about this. The tone is oppositional. The Lord is king, not that guy sitting on the throne in Jerusalem ... or wherever. The Lord is president, not the one sitting in the oval office, but the Lord God who created us all.

Now we're saying something. In a world of competing interests and loyalties we are being clear. When push comes to shove, we stand with God and no other. When the laws of God and the laws of human beings are in conflict with one another we will follow the laws of God, no matter what the cost. God is our king! God alone is holy!

This psalm, it turns out, is a sort of political manifesto. This God is not only president. This God loves justice and will establish it as [he] brings equity to all people! This is the God we choose to follow in baptism. This is the God we claim as we embrace the Son, Jesus Christ. This God is our president, and no other.

Now before the critiques start flying, it's important to note that this is no call for some theistic anarchy. There is a place for worldly leaders. We need hospitals, schools, and roads. We need good government to make sure that all the people have enough to eat and that true justice lives in the land. However, as we assert this need for reasonable human leadership, let us be clear. Our final allegiance is to God and God alone. "Extol the Lord our God and worship at his holy mountain, for the Lord our God is holy."

137

Psalm 99

Former Secretary of Education, Richard Riley, once remarked that "We are the victims of the tyranny of lowered expectations." Secretary Riley went on to say that as a people, we have flattened out our expectations into a broad and bland sense of mediocrity. We, too, often settle for below average performance or something that we deem as "good enough." Rarely, if ever, do we call for — much less demand — excellence. Excellence, it seems, is not an option in our world today. Indeed, go to any public school and observe the treatment received by an "A" student at the hands of his or her peers. Ridicule, shunning, and even violence await those who excel.

Perhaps it is the mentality of the lowest common denominator at work. Fearful of being surpassed or failing, the crowd will attack and bring down any among it who show signs of moving ahead. Or maybe it is a misguided sense of democracy. Frequently in community settings, the lifting up of excellence is discouraged because it might make others feel badly. Instead, everyone gets the award — so that no one might lose. But there is a sinister truth underlying all this. And that is that when everyone is excellent, there is no excellence.

In such a repressed environment as this, how are the people to consider a thing such as holiness? If greatness and creativity are not encouraged among the people, how then can the people perceive the greatness and creativity of their God? Holiness, after all, means something that is other than, or apart from, the common. God is holy because God isn't you or me. God is holy because ... as scripture reminds us, God is ... God.

In the muddied waters of modernity, what passes for holy these days? How is it that the people experience awe? What, aside from the next acquisition, gets the attention of people these days? At the risk of walking unsupported onto a fragile limb, this writer will suggest that in our dumbed down, numbed out mass consciousness we have lost the ability to perceive excellence. Worse still, we have ceased to yearn for it.

In days gone by, much effort was given to ridiculing the blandness of socialist culture. Unimaginative architecture, state controlled art, and tightly restricted education all lent to the fall of a once grand and idealistic system. But the question comes today to each one of us. Where is excellence? Of what — or whom — do we stand in awe? How do we find the holiness of God, and therefore the excellence to which each person is called?

Perhaps a new beginning might be made in the reading of this psalm as we claim without reservation the utter holiness of God. Perhaps, as we pause in awe of God, we might begin the work of becoming the people of God's dreams, a people committed to wonder, to awe, to excellence in every endeavor we undertake.

Psalm 100

In a world where relativity seems to have taken over, clarity feels good. In a culture where good and evil are mushed together into a stew of cynical apathy, the simple declaration of a truth has a cleansing and revitalizing effect. "Old 100," as past generations have called this psalm, takes on this task with wonderful success.

No equivocation is allowed. No standing on the sidelines will be tolerated. No half-baked, vague spirituality will suffice. Those who have contented themselves with a quiescent, noncommittal faith are called out of the shadows of complacency. Every one, even the entire earth, is compelled to make a joyful noise to the Lord. Imagine the cacophony! The stamping of a thousand feet; the shrieking of youthful voices; the impromptu swaying of wild dancers; the soaring wail of a wall of voices singing at the top of the lungs; all of it given over to worshiping the God of Israel, the Lord who comes to us in Jesus Christ.

This is worship beyond liturgy. This is praise beyond planning. This is the glorification of God that arises from spirits set afire by the Holy Spirit. It is a holy moment. For all at once it dawns upon the people. This is the creator God, the God who made us. This is the God who numbers the hairs on our heads and places the beating heart within us. This is the God who rescues us in times of trouble. This is the God who saves! We throw our lot in with this God and declare that we belong to this God. If we are a people, we are God's people. We live out our lives on the planet and in the pastures that this God made.

This last part of the psalm is as powerful as the first words, and it calls to mind a typical Sunday morning. Enter the church with thanksgiving and the fellowship hall with praise! Invite all the neighbors to a sacred potluck! March down the aisle with hands waving and hearts held high. Wouldn't that be a sight to behold? Imagine churches everywhere breaking out in songs of thanksgiving and a fellowship of praise! It would be a revolution of praise, an uprising of thanksgiving, a moment of utter and complete clarity.

Psalm 100

"Know that the Lord is God! It is [God] who made us, and we are [God's]" (v. 3). In an age of extreme individualism, the idea that human beings belong to God is not only anachronistic, it borders on the offensive. The response is almost automatic. "What? Me? Belong to someone? Never! I am my own man ... or woman!" Contemporary culture is obsessed with the notion that each individual person is in charge of their own destiny. It is rife with the fiction that each person is a unique entity making choices only for themselves, and it is only to themselves that they owe loyalty or fealty.

Evidence of this malaise can be seen in the decline of voluntarism and charitable giving, as well as in the unwillingness of a whole generation to "join" anything, much less a church. In church circles, one can see this as people engaging in a consumer-based approach to church life. If the poor pastor provides what the people want, then they stay and make their contributions. If the clergyman or clergywoman does not meet the felt needs of the people, then they go someplace where those alleged needs will be met. Where, in this mix, is the call of faithfulness to God?

"Old 100" pulls us back to the truth that we do belong to God. We are, as the psalm clearly articulates, God's people and no other. We are sheep in whose pasture? God's! This is weighty stuff in today's culture, and it will take some courageous leadership if this notion is to be reclaimed in the life of faith.

In spite of the endless barrage of information that insists on the opposite, it turns out that there is something bigger than our own individual wants and desires. It turns out that the search to discern and do God's will is the path to which people of faith are called. In this call is the fundamental understanding that we belong — not to ourselves or any organization or clan — we are answerable, not to our own whims and desires or to any power or authority other than that of God our creator and redeemer.

It is for this reason that our sense of confession begins, not with a laundry list of mistakes, missteps, and misdeeds, but rather with the simple openhearted declaration, "The Lord is God. It is [God] who made us, and we belong to [God]. We are [God's] people, the sheep of [God's] pasture" (v. 3).

Psalm 104:1-9, 24, 35c

The voice of praise rings beautifully through this psalm as each verse gives poetic color to the glories of creation and its maker. It is something to be read and re-read as we contemplate the wonders of God.

Somehow, though, our modern sensibilities rest a little uneasily with such boundless enthusiasm. We squirm a bit and shyly point out that such praise comes from a less complicated day and age. When life was less tarnished by the barrage of culture it was easier to rely upon a creator God such as the one described here. Today, however, people of faith must contend with the floodwaters of a culture that has packaged and marketed God for its own convenience. Today, the faithful spend their life's energy fending off the commodification of just about everything and everyone. In times like these, such childlike praise seems imprudent. In our day of critical examination and cynical distrust, such unchecked praise is suspect.

This is why multiple readings of this psalm are required. Once, twice, three times or more, read it aloud. Mantric and prayerful, allow each phrase to roll from the mouth in spirited utterance. Each reading strips away a little more veneer. Each phrase of praise gets the reader a little closer to a truth too well hidden. This truth was known by the writer of this psalm and is known still in various corners of the larger faith community.

This truth is the liberating and world shattering notion that we human beings are not in charge. There is something bigger and more powerful than us. There is someone who sets boundaries that we dare not cross.

Such truth-telling confronts human beings with the fact that we, as a species, have what pop psychology might label as "boundary issues." Before a God who created us, we chafe at the idea that there might some things we ought not do. We smirk at the concept that a boundary set by God is not something to be automatically violated, but something to be respected. Part of that respect is reclaimed in the childlike act of praise as we read and pray this psalm.

The words, "Bless the Lord O my soul" are far more than lip service paid in a vapid Call to Worship on Sunday morning. This is a voice that comes from the depths of one's person. God is offered praise and blessing from the heart, from the inner core, from ... the soul!

Psalm 104:24-34, 35b

"Yonder is the sea, great and wide!" The beach is the perfect place to get in touch with the grandeur of God's creative wonder. Preferably, this is a beach with few sunbathers and fewer skimpy bathing suits. Free of such distraction, the timeless rhythm of the waves can work its way into the soul. Pressing bare feet into ever-changing but ever-similar sand reminds the spirit that God, too, is ever-changing yet always the same. The salt scent of the breeze moves the spirit into an ancient, primal place and calls the heart to see God's Spirit hovering over the waters at the beginning of creation. And the horizon? That shifting line where sky and sea meld into one is a resting and birthing place for vision and hope. It pulls scattered thoughts toward a focused and sacred future, and it leaves a tainted past behind.

It's a good thing to stop once in a while to drink in the amazing wonders of God. It doesn't need to be the beach, of course. Ohio or Missouri work well, too. As this psalm so beautifully suggests, the location doesn't matter. It could be the mountains, the plains, or even a small town in upstate New York. God's incredible, life-giving Spirit is everywhere. And it is powerfully evident as we survey the wonders of creation.

Wherever you are, what's important is not so much the address you type into your GPS. What matters is the stopping. What matters is the complete halt to business as usual. What matters is that moment one takes to drink in unspeakable glories of God.

Without that pause, life becomes a whirlwind of doing. Without that simple break to take it all in, minutes and hours suddenly turn into a lifetime passed without the life-giving touch of wonder. How tragic to see a life come to a close when that life has been void of wonder.

Perhaps this psalm can serve as a summons. Could it be that this psalm embodies a call for people of faith to participate in a conspiracy of wonder? Is it possible that each person is called to be a missionary of God's wonder?

Do you know someone who is overly busy? Do you know someone too focused on work? Do you know someone caught in anger or cynicism? Help them to stop. Take them to the beach. Walk with them through a field. Brew them a cup of coffee.

Take a moment. Take this moment and use it to spread God's wonder wherever you are in whatever way you can.

Psalm 104:24-34, 35b

In Christian tradition, we receive the gift of the Holy Spirit as a partner on the journey (John 14:16; 15:26; 16:7), an advocate who will accompany us on our journey toward faithfulness. We hear the Pentecost story and delight in the dancing tongues of fire as they descend and create something new in their wake.

On Pentecost, we celebrate not only the arrival of the advocate, but quite literally, the creation of Christian community as the Spirit enlivens and creates. As we claim anew this Spirit, as we celebrate this powerful gift, this psalm serves to remind us of the creative power of God's Spirit. "When you send forth your Spirit, they are created." The psalmist, of course, is speaking about the "creeping things innumerable," that give testimony to God's greatness.

The point we are to take away with us is that it is God's Spirit that creates. It is God's Spirit that came as "a wind from God, sweeping over the face of the water" (Genesis 1:2). And it is God's Spirit that literally creates Christian community.

Just as that Spirit formed the oceans and the land, it forms us in community. Just as that Spirit created the countless forms of creatures and life, it creates us in the warp and woof of living community.

No wonder there are so many references in scripture to creation and new beginnings (such as 2 Corinthians 5:17; Galatians 6:15) as the early church struggled to find its feet! No wonder we see Jesus as a kind of new Adam (see Romans 5:14; 1 Corinthians 15:45). It is the power and the wonder of the Holy Spirit creating Christian community much in the same way that that self-same Spirit created the world!

The coming of the Holy Spirit on Pentecost is no less an event of significance, then, than the creation of the world. If we could embrace that power of this notion, how might it change the way in which we approach and participate in our church communities? Perhaps on this Pentecost Day we might make a new start at treasuring *both* of God's creations. Perhaps we might reach out to halt the destruction of the earth and learn to treasure it more as stewards and caretakers than as owners and dominators. And then, perhaps we might also learn how to better treasure and care for that second creation: the gift of Christian community.

Psalm 104:24-34, 35b

Today is Pentecost. The creative power of God's Spirit (v. 30) flows today like no other day. The Spirit that is poured out on this day is the same Spirit that hovered over the waters (Genesis 1:2) at the dawn of creation. This is the same Spirit that possessed Gideon as he lifted up his horn (Judges 6:4). And it is the same Spirit that the risen Jesus told us would arrive as an advocate to accompany us (John 14:16) forever.

This Spirit that gives life, that motivates, that creates and accompanies comes on us today, drawing us together in the heat of creative fire. This is no trifling wind, no puffed up breath or gasbag of religious meandering. This is God's Spirit. It is real. It is not limited like human doctrine. It is not to be contained like a restless adolescent. This wonderful, chaotic, and Holy Spirit goes where it will, and today it comes to this place.

For those who lean into a well-ordered life this Spirit can be troubling. For those who like a tidy religion, this Spirit can be downright disruptive. New life can be that way. Creativity can be that way, especially when it's God who's getting creative!

So it is that today as God's torrent of life flows out in dancing tongues of fire, we are called to lay down our need to control what's happening. Remember that it was so out of control on Pentecost that folks thought everyone was drunk! *No, no, not drunk*, says Peter, *but ripe with visions and dreams, full of power and imagination!*

And it is to us that the question comes today. Are we ready for God's disturbing Spirit to enter our lives? Are we ready to let go of our need to control, to order, and to organize? Can we surrender it all and allow God's spiritual fire to consume us as it did our ancestors so long ago?

Imagine, just for a moment, what it would mean to be consumed by this holy fire. What would that mean? What would our lives look like if they were utterly given over to the whimsy of God's wonderful Spirit? It is at once a thrilling and terrifying notion. Thrilling because of the liberation that would come as each heart was released of every burden and freed for faithfulness. Terrifying because it would mean that life as we know it would be over. Those things that we hold so close would be laid upon the pyre for burning and we would — whether we want to admit it or not — feel bereft.

It is Pentecost Day, a spiritual time of adventure and disarray. It is also a time of deep prayer and unutterable joy. It is a time to dance to the rhythm of the Spirit's flame.

Psalm 105:1-6, 16-22, 45b

Sometimes it's hard to keep the big picture in mind. When the exigencies of the present moment conspire against us it's nearly impossible to look past the current struggle. Whether it's an argument with one's spouse or a disagreement at work, most people find themselves caught up in the heat of what's going on and forget — too often — that there are bigger things at stake. Often, in moments like this, well-intentioned individuals earn our anger when they remark that God has a higher purpose in mind or comment that what's taking place in the moment is "God's will." Imagine saying to someone like Joseph that his enslavement is part of God's plan.

The whole question is a thorny one. If God has some huge master plan in which every person is playing a part, then how do we deal with the likes of Adolf Hitler or with the story of human slavery in the Americas? To make it more personal, how does a pastor tell a grieving mother that her son's death in a gang shooting is part of the bigger picture? How indeed?

The question lifts up ways of viewing God's presence among us. The first is an image of God as master puppeteer. In this vision, which it would seem our psalm supports, God manages the universe down to every last detail and calls upon the people to trust that the end result is in God's hands. The second vision involves a creator God who has given the people "free will" and called them into relationship with "him." In this vision, it's not God, but we who are the masters of our fate. Here, God did not initiate the holocaust, human beings did. God did not pull the trigger on the gun that cut a young man's life short, a human being did.

The challenge to human understanding in this context is to engage a God who is all powerful while also engaging a God who gifted us with free will. It seems that the understanding of this psalm might be found at the nexus of this challenge. It should also be pointed out that this understanding dances back and forth between one's sense of the immediate and one's ability to see a bigger picture.

When kidnapped and sold into slavery, can anyone maintain a sense of the bigger picture? When cradling the lifeless form of

146

your son in your arms, can you think about God's providence? Perhaps such a view is better seen through the lens of time passed. Certainly, these concerns can be better unfolded in forums more substantial than this. But whether it's Joseph sold into slavery or any one of countless circumstances crying out for understanding, these questions will always live at the core of our faith.

Psalm 105:1-6, 23-26, 45c

The power of these words is rooted in memory. The remembering of God's mighty works is basis for praise. The remembering of the salvation story gives light to future generations. Indeed, as we move beyond the psalms to Christian scripture and its derivative faith, we are called to remember as we celebrate the sacrament of holy communion. Memory, it seems, is the key to the whole enterprise of faith. More than this, memory is important to the advancement of civilization, even one could say, to the survival of the human species.

If we don't remember and retell the stories, our faith will disappear. It is much the same within civilization. Remembering the primary stories of a culture insures its survival. And even down to the survival of the species, memory is crucial. Remembering, for example, where the cave bears dwell was key in the survival of ancient humans. Yes, memory is a foundation stone of human reality.

Memory, however, is not static. It lives and moves and breathes. Memory is like a snowball rolled down a hill. It acquires new snow with rotation downward, growing larger and larger. In fact, memory also depends upon new acquisition as time goes forward. Without new experiences, both individual and corporate memory would become stale and brittle.

An interesting exercise might be for a congregation or faith community to think and pray about the new things taking place that they would like to remember. What dynamic and powerful things are happening in ministry? Mission? Evangelism? What things add snow to the rolling ball of faith as it hurtles down the hill? What new elements give vibrancy and power to the memories they will pass on to another generation?

147

And if, as may be the case in some communities, there are no new memories to add to this snowball, there is a challenge to be met. What new things might be undertaken that would be memorable? What ministries might ignite a community to move forward? What new enterprise might unite and give power?

Memory is indeed important. But if it is not fed with the new power and energy of experience, it will simply grow stale and brittle and will surely shatter on its way down the hill.

Psalm 105:1-6, 37-45

Here is a psalm, like many, which leans into praise and rejoicing. We are called to sing and to tell out the wonderful works of God. It is a call, especially to those who are seeking. "Let the hearts of those who seek the Lord rejoice." "Seek the Lord, and his strength...."

It is an interesting hiccup here to notice that those who seek are called to rejoice. Usually the popular mind assumes that those who rejoice are the ones who have found and experienced the Lord. Yet, here we find an out-and-out call to go ahead and "seek the Lord." One could, without much imagination, put forth the argument here that God — or those seeking God — are lost a good chunk of the time.

Why would someone who hasn't found something wish to rejoice? Having spent the better part of a morning looking for keys, this writer can tell you that the seeking is not much fun at all, and that rejoicing was the furthest thing from thought or intention. Yet, even in the contemporary world, seekers seem to get a lot of attention. There are worship services oriented to "seekers." There are whole conferences teaching pastors and lay leaders how to be "seeker sensitive." What is going on with all this, anyway? What about those who have found it? Don't they deserve some attention?

The whole discussion brings to mind a T-shirt seen at a youth rally lately. It said, in crazy comic lettering, "The journey is my home." Is it possible that there is another path between those who have "found it," and those who ... have not? What if the faded, multicolored T-shirt raised the same point that this psalm subtly asserts? What if the journey *is* our home?

What if finding God is not a process with a finite end point but a way of being alive? What if God is so holy, so awesome, so huge, and so infinite that even if one seeks a lifetime there will only be momentary flashes of brilliance and gasps of sudden revelation?

If this is the case, and this brief missive would offer that perhaps it is, what does this do with all of our religious trappings and doctrine? If we are called to a lifetime of seeking after the holy, how do we address those who believe they have it all locked and finalized?

Perhaps the answer is as simple as the psalm suggests. Just praise the Lord and keep on seeking.

Psalm 105:1-11, 45b

One hears much these days about "seekers." The word in contemporary usage usually refers to people who are vaguely spiritual in nature but have not managed to focus on a particular tradition or practice. These wandering souls are much sought after by churches these days. There are Seeker Worship Services, Seeker Discussion Groups, Seeker Suppers, and even Seeker Singles Groups. Within the confines of these groups one often hears people self-described as "spiritual." Often someone will say, "I'm very spiritual, but I'm not into organized religion."

The ready wit always responds to this, saying, "You don't like organized religion? Brother, you've come to the right church! We're anything but organized here!" But in truth there is something unsettling and unspoken behind this dislike of so-called organized religion.

It is, candidly, a form of spiritual laziness. Spirituality requires more than a romantic walk on the beach. It is deeper than an infatuation with shallow wanderings into the antechambers of the great religious traditions. Any spirituality requires discipline. Whether it is Buddhist, Hindu, Jewish, Islam, or Christian matters not. Any serious pursuit of spirituality requires discipline, and, yes

... organization. No one would think to pick up a Stradivarius violin and play it like a master without decades of practice. Not just anyone can mount the stage with a professional ballet company and dance as well as the members of the company. Indeed, these concepts are almost humorous to us. We understand that years and years of practice are necessary to achieve mastery in the arts. Yet somehow we assume that a person can simply "be spiritual" by merely stating the case.

A true seeker after the holy engages a rigorous discipline of prayer, meditation, and living. It isn't a hobby or a pastime. It is a way of life. It is this kind of seeking that these verses in Psalm 105 address. To "seek God's presence continually," is to focus and engage. It is to set aside the ego and the fleeting desires of our own daily lives and give one's self over to the seeking. For us, this search involves singing God's praises and calling out God's name. It leads us to remembering God's mighty works and to continually keeping ourselves open to the leading of God's Spirit.

As churches across the land try to open their doors to "seekers," one avenue might be to invite people into the disciplines of spirituality. Instead of lowering the bar so that anyone can merely step into spirituality's realm, perhaps the best idea is to raise that same bar and invite everyone into excellence and wonder. It might just be that the key to reviving the church is found in claiming spiritual practice and discipline. It might just be that this is the call of the church in a new time.

Psalm 106:1-6, 19-23

The opening lines of this psalm proclaim the love of God that is both trustworthy and lasting. It's not only lasting, it's permanent. In a world where human relationships are pretty much disposable, the notion of trusting, permanent love registers somewhere in the mind as a fantasy. With many people on third and fourth marriages, lifelong commitment is just not seen as real. In a world where markets and profitability have overruled morality, friendships fall to the dictates of making money and maintaining one's job. In the midst of it all, relationships of every kind suffer because, quite candidly, people simply do not wish to do the hard work it takes to maintain them.

From families to school chums, to siblings and colleagues, relationships are simply not given a high priority in contemporary culture. How then are the people to understand a God who loves them not only with integrity, but loves them forever? Such a concept leaves people either scoffing or in muted awe. But there it is.

The whole Judeo-Christian heritage is rooted in the reality of a God who loves faithfully and forever. It is, in fact, our interaction with this God that makes up the meat and marrow of our story. We are who we are because of lasting and committed love. In fact, it could be said that our whole existence is owed to a love like this.

God loves us steadfastly and forever! This is particularly astonishing when we consider that God knows everything — everything about us. This has to be terrifying to most of us. Anyone reading these words keeps secrets about themselves. We believe, perhaps rightly, that if anyone actually knew everything about us then we would not be loved. So we keep secrets and carefully dole out information about ourselves in a way that will present a view of ourselves that is easy to love. But God knows it all. Every deep, dark, little thing God knows. God knows all about you and loves you all the way. Astonishing indeed.

How do we comprehend a love like this? How do we embrace a love like this? It is overwhelming even to think about it. Perhaps a good first step might be to lay down all the pretending illusions we make up about ourselves because ... this God already knows about our silly smoke and mirrors act. This God knows and loves.

After laying it all down and standing before God just as we are, maybe we can reach out and receive this incredible steadfast and forever love.

Psalm 107:1-3, 17-22

It's been said that people have short memories. It must be so. Simple observation is verification enough. Many can site the passage of time as reason enough. Middle age slips barely noticed into old age. Memories blend and soon come the moments when the reason for walking into a room are unclear. Collectively, we forget the lessons of history, as war after war scars the face of God. Acts of tyrants and lunatics conveniently slip the common mind as the tape loop of history plays again and again. Same story, different characters.

These slippages are troubling, it's true, but there is a deeper, more profound memory loss that plagues us. We forget, as this writer points out, our God who has done great things for us.

For the people of Israel, it was forgetting the great liberation of the exodus. "The wondrous works in the land of Ham, and awesome deeds by the Red Sea" (vv. 21-22). This is significant. It's rather like forgetting the name of your mother or father.

Before we get too judgmental with the people of Israel, though, we ought to take a look at ourselves. Confession, it turns out, really is good for the soul. The question to be posed here is not if we have forgotten God, but how. A look at our behavior, particularly within churches, indicates painfully our ecclesial loss of memory.

Are our sanctuaries truly what they claim to be? Safe places? Sanctuaries in deed and not just in name? Have we "broken down the dividing wall, that is, the hostility between us"? (Ephesians 2:14). Or do we make distinctions and judgments, pushing the very people from us whom God calls us to welcome and to love? Have we forgotten the God who calls us into "ministries of reconciliation"? (2 Corinthians 5:16). Do we recall the Savior who gave it all so that we might claim a new life of hope and justice?

These are not trivial questions. Think about our churches. Consider your own church. Is the Christian community a place where God is recalled and honored, both in individual and communal lives, or is God neatly tucked into the shadows of institutional necessities?

Just as people with no vision will surely perish, so too will the faith community that does not keep the saving God at the core of their being. Church budgets, council meetings, and the chatter of the institution may feel important, but it can all become an easy occasion for idolatry (vv. 19-20).

152

It falls to each of us, then, to remember God, not as an act of sentimental recollection, but as the Savior who comes always into our lives to call us to faithfulness. The creating one who is worthy of our worship, our praise, and yes, our obedience.

Psalm 107:1-7, 33-37

Steadfastness (v. 1) is not a concept that carries well into contemporary culture. The notion of a love that endures forever would leave many people glancing upward with a cynical eye. It's true. Nearly half of all marriages end in divorce. Some studies suggest that in those marriages that do last, infidelity runs, once again near half. Families are scattered far and wide, rendering lifelong enduring relationships difficult at best. Friendships, too, suffer from a world in which all things and people are viewed as disposable commodities.

Aging men dispose of wives and search out younger women in order to stave off the march of time. Women, too, cast off husbands in search of something that seems to be missing. Relationships of all sorts are torn apart by contemporary life. From the stress of ideology to the burdens of economy and back again, relationships are left behind like corpses on the field of battle. It is not merely our interpersonal relationships that are problematic. The civic contract in the larger community is frayed, as well. Government leaders routinely lie, dragging whole nations into war and ruin. Hopelessness and fear mark the rhythm of days as disempowered people stand and watch the hapless erosion of civil and human rights.

In the midst of such fickle human connections, how is it that the claims of a steadfast God can be realized? In the turmoil of human faithlessness, how do we reach for a God who we are told will not go away? Indeed, there are precious few human examples and no ready answer except this. Steadfast love is based on trust, and trust can only form when fear has fled.

It seems that letting go of fear is the primary task. However, it is not likely that such release can be undertaken by any one individual. Perhaps the riddle is answered in the New Testament letter

153

of 1 John. Here, as in virtually no other place in scripture, God is actually defined. We are told that "God is love," and that "perfect love casts out fear." So it is in our brokenness that we are introduced to a new symbiotic relationship. In utter faithfulness God reaches always for us. Some would call this grace. If we respond to such reaching, our fears are relieved and we are launched into a new life of love and trust. Yes — there is risk — but in reaching for a God who already reaches for you, such risk shrinks as grace grows and fear recedes. It is at least worth a try.

Psalm 107:1-9, 43

"Let the redeemed of the Lord say so!" How often do we give credit where it's due? As a younger pastor serving in New York City, one of the more intense church arguments I remember having was over a bag lunch program the church was sponsoring. Every Sunday following worship, the members of the church would gather and make a couple of hundred bag lunches. Nothing fancy — sandwiches, fruit, a cookie or two, and something to drink. Then the congregation would head into a nearby park where a host of homeless people spent their days, and we would give them the lunches.

The argument wasn't over whether or not to do this. There was no debate about the ministry at all, except this one thing. The pastor wanted to slip a note in each bag saying, "This lunch was brought to you with the love of Jesus Christ by the people of Washington Square Church."

Some folks thought we shouldn't put our name or any notice in the bags. We should just do anonymous good and be pleased with that. Others, including the pastor, thought it important that the folks receiving the lunches knew both the why and the wherefore. The debate was spirited, and ultimately the name did go into the bag lunches. But the whole discussion recalls this passage from the psalm.

It's a good question, and one that any congregation might take up as an afternoon discussion. Are we the redeemed of the Lord? If redemption through God's love is something that has been experienced in one's life, then it seems only reasonable that it should be

154

shared. If our very spirit has been renewed, our hearts transformed; if we have been saved, redeemed by God, then shouldn't the people who have received such an incredible blessing be willing, not just to "say so," but to shout it from the rooftops?

So many church members attend faithfully every Sunday but rarely discuss or share anything about their faith with friends or coworkers during the week. Why is that? Shyness? Fear of giving offense? Perhaps a bit of both. But in the end, the logic of it all seems so clear.

Let us give credit where credit is due. If God has touched your life; if the Holy Spirit has come and inhabited your heart, then by all means, say so!

Psalm 111

Convincing someone of an idea is not an easy task. Anyone who has worked in politics can vouch for this. Teachers, preachers, community leaders, all know how hard it is to convince people to rally behind an idea or a concept. Harder still, is the effort to get people to act on something.

There is, however, one magic trick that works almost every time, and that is *fear*. As German writer Bertolt Brecht put it: "Magic fear puts the world at your command!" A people who are afraid will do most anything. Adolf Hitler knew this very well, as he brilliantly manipulated and manufactured a fear of Jews. Countless leaders, both religious and political, have relied on this magic fear for centuries. From fomenting fears of Christians in the Roman Empire to stirring up fear of "terrorists" today, the manipulation of people through fear continues unabated.

Upon reading this psalm, one might get the idea that the fear game is being played here as well. We praise God, the psalm asserts, for all of God's mighty works. But in the end, it's because of fear that God gives food (v. 5). Moreover, fear of God is the "beginning of wisdom."

The evidence is strong. Follow God, or else. Indeed, it causes shudders down the spine to imagine how our ancestors in the faith made use of such fear.

However, it's worth noting that the translators of holy scriptures have made a bit of a slip here. It seems that the Hebrew words that have been translated into the English word "fear," do not in fact *mean* "fear." In both cases a more accurate translation would be "reverence."

It doesn't take a rocket scientist to notice that there's a good bit of distance between "fear" and "reverence." A given person or people may well do something as a result of being made afraid. However, true reverence arises from a different location.

It is reverence that gives this psalm its depth and beauty, not fear. Praising God because of God's wonderful works is something we can manage. Who can stand on top of Half Dome at Yosemite and not feel reverence? Falling down in worship because of God's faithfulness to the covenant is something we can get our minds and hearts around. It is not so hard to revere a God who will not abandon us.

While our traditions, both religious and political, opt too often for fear as a primary motivator, might we perhaps take a step toward reverence? Worship and praise induced by a humble acknowledgment of God's utter greatness will lead us in a very different direction than praise motivated by fear. Let us begin together by pausing to revere our God in worship and in the rest of our lives.

Psalm 111

"The fear of the Lord is the beginning of wisdom" (v. 10). "Perfect love casts out fear" (1 John 4:18). These two powerful statements reveal for us the inadequacies of the translation process of the English language. These two juxtaposing passages reveal only a tiny fraction of the contradictions and conflicts found within our holy Word. No wonder people have trouble reading and understanding.

The fear of God mentioned in this psalm is not the same fear that is cast out by love. A more appropriate translation of this fear might be to understand it as awe. So it is then that "awe of the Lord is the beginning of wisdom." That works. Awe, you see, includes a healthy bit of fear but it is more than that. Awe is that realization that someone or something is so far beyond us that all we can do is stop and quietly stare with mouths open in respectful silence. Awe blends fear with admiration and respect. It is the total admission that someone or something is superior to us. And yes, when it comes to God, awe is the beginning of wisdom.

The fear that casts out love, on the other hand, is different. The Greek root for this is *phobos*. Our English word, "phobia," comes from here. This is the kind of fear that renders people impotent and paralyzed. It is the kind of fear nurtured and fed by entities interested in controlling people. German writer Bertolt Brecht once remarked, "Magic fear puts the world at your command!" When people are scared, they will submit to a great deal if they think it will keep them safe. All one needs to do is to look at the history of this nation over the past few years to find confirmation of this.

Different from awe, this fear is not helpful and does need to be cast away from us. Perfect love, or agape, is the answer. Love engendered and nourished in the context of Christian community can, and does, banish this fear. In a community that understands the need to create a safe place for peoples' spirits, emotions, and bodies, fear will dissipate. In a community rooted in the Holy Spirit and leaning into God's healing grace, fear will fade into the holy qualities of trust, Spirit-led affection, and hope. And it's funny that all of this begins really with that first kind of fear — or awe — that leads to wisdom. Full circle. Full hope. Fullness of God's presence.

Psalm 114

This psalm calls up some wonderful imagery. Occasioned by the "presence of God," the sea looks up and flees. The personification is beautiful, if a bit damp in the execution. One conjures up an image of a whole ocean looking up, noticing God, and then taking the first train out of town. It is only with eyes closed and imagination flowing that one can see whole mountains skipping like rams through a spring-flowered field.

Such pictures are joyful and whimsical. They burst the boundaries of what is thought to be possible and paint magical triptychs of what happens when God's presence is perceived and embraced.

157

This all begs the question of human response to God's presence. If oceans can flee and mountains can dance, what can human beings do once God's presence is a part of their reality? If earth itself can tremble and rocks can be transformed into water, what then can women and men do if they are mindful of God's presence?

Is it conceivable that, mindful of God's presence, human beings could put an end to war and poverty? That would certainly trump dancing mountains and fleeing oceans. Is it even thinkable that, engaged in the presence of God, humankind could heal diseases and bring equity to our social order?

It seems that the critical element here is an awareness of, or engagement in, the presence of God. Can humans take this step? Can awareness of the divine penetrate our notoriously thick heads? Can the overwhelming power of God's loving presence pierce our well-armored hearts? Perhaps it would be easier to imagine mountains dancing.

Yet, isn't the possibility of such things a stimulant to the mind? Don't the images of this psalm provoke our visionary spirits and knock at the doors of shuttered courage? God can unleash the sense of what is possible and shove us into a new realm of being. God can open the eyes of our heart and ignite the fires of passion.

Sensitive to and mindful of God's presence, human beings could transform the face of the globe. The destruction of the environment could be halted and reversed. Ancient hatreds could be overcome and transformed into loving partnerships.

It's not too late. Let this psalm issue the call for humankind to open their hearts, their eyes, and their spirits to the reality of God's presence. Let this psalm paint the portrait of a God-engaged people. And let the dancing of the mountains begin!

Psalm 116:1-2, 12-19

"I owe you one." These words came out of my mouth only yesterday as a church member graciously agreed to attend a meeting in my stead. Indeed, it was a generous thing and a debt is outstanding indeed. This debt, of course, is likely to be paid through a pleasant lunch or some other social interaction. But here is a debt of altogether different proportions.

How does one repay God for the countless blessings that God provides? I recently visited Lake Tahoe and was stunned by the beauty even as I quipped to a colleague that I thought it was some of God's best work. Best work indeed — it was breathtakingly beautiful. When one considers the awesome things God has done, how can payback even take shape in one's mind? What does that look like?

The quick and nimble pastor would raise a hand and mention tithing. Others of lesser moral standing might turn such indebtedness to the service of nationalism. "Look how God has blessed our nation! Shouldn't you do thus and such for us in return?" Usually, this involves picking up a gun and shooting strangers.

But still the question stands: What will it look like when we "offer a thanksgiving of sacrifice"?

The word "sacrifice" is a pretty big clue. This means that it should cost us something. Our payback to God ought not be like a waiter's tip at the local diner or the few quarters we throw hurriedly at the bum on the street corner with an empty coffee cup. No, this giving of thanks is to be substantive.

Some offer up their lives. Mother Teresa, Dorothy Day, and Daniel Berrigan come readily to mind, and few of us could measure up to these oaks of righteousness. But still, a life offered in thanksgiving is no small thing. Others offer time and talent. Still others give fortunes while others spend lives in prayer, and as a parish pastor I dare not miss that call to tithing. It really does make a difference.

In the end, everyone will make their own decisions about such things. Whatever shape the offering takes; however it is we construct our efforts to give back, it should in all ways be undertaken with a sense of wonder and gratitude. For truly, this is a marvelous God who hears our voices and "inclines his ear to us."

Psalm 116:1-2, 12-19

In the United States of America today, the average household carries a credit card debt load of several thousand dollars. If you include auto loans and mortgage into the mix, the total shoots much higher than that. If you multiply this amount by the millions of households the amount of indebtedness is staggering. Then, of course, we look to the government. Here, the debt is beyond one's ability to imagine. Paying for war is not only expensive, it has plunged this nation into billions of dollars of debt — most of which is owed to other nations.

As a people floundering in debt, this psalm offers an interesting note to reflect upon. It casts the relationship we have with the holy as one where the writer is in a position of "paying back the Lord for all (his) bounty." As far as credit cards and auto loans go, we know how to pay those back — though perhaps we procrastinate and go deeper still into debt as we make minimum payments and negative amortization mortgages.

But how is it that we repay God?

The quick thinking pastor, of course, will pull out a pledge card and ask the feckless parishioner to give a tithe. Ten percent up front, and there is, of course, biblical precedent for this (see Deuteronomy 26:12). And yes, everyone should tithe to their church!

However, this psalm, and this writer suspects that it doesn't end with the monthly tithe check. As one church treasurer wryly asserted, "If you think you're in debt to the credit card company, think about the debt you owe God." Indeed, everything belongs to God. This is why Jesus could so winningly acquiesce to his questioners on the issue of taxes (Matthew 22:15-22). He, like any good Jew of his day, was quite aware that everything belongs to God. So when he said to give Caesar what belonged to him, it was with no small amount of irony. Nothing belongs to Caesar. Everything belongs to God! The psalmist understands this at the deepest level and pledges fidelity and full payment. Still, the question of means of payment remains unanswered.

Perhaps the answer for Christians today is best found in Romans 12:1. "I appeal to you therefore, brothers and sisters, by the mercies of God, to present your bodies as a living sacrifice, holy and acceptable to God, which is your spiritual worship." In other words, the gift of sacrifice that God wants is our lives lived faithfully according to God's word. As we sit and remember the sacrifice made for us in the Holy Week, is anything less than this acceptable?

Psalm 116:1-2, 12-19

The words of this psalm emerge from a grateful heart. They flow from the consciousness of one who knows the saving power of God in concrete terms. More to the point, they reflect the experience of someone who has been rescued. Public safety professionals experience this kind of thing frequently. In the daily line of their work they rescue people, and the gratefulness of some of them is remarkable. A woman whose children have been rescued from a fire shows up at the fire station every week with gifts for the firefighters. She falls all over herself thanking them again and again. She becomes a booster for the fire station, raising funds and developing community support. She even remembers the rescuers in her will. This is the kind of gratefulness that flows from this psalm.

Here we have more than brave firefighters on the job. Here we have God as the rescuer.

In a culture where privilege and entitlement are the prevailing sentiments of the day, this is a hard thing to grasp. Most people can't imagine that they need rescuing, so being grateful for such a rescue isn't really within their emotional vocabulary. Yet the truth is that we do need rescuing. We need rescuing from this epidemic of consumerism, which is strangling our spirit and ruining the life of the planet. We need rescuing from the blindness that keeps us from being sensitive to the suffering of others. We need to be rescued from our participation in the wounding and death of millions of innocent people. There is no question about it. We're in trouble. Whether we wish to acknowledge it or not, we are a people who need rescuing. We are a people who need God.

The incredible part of it all is that our rescuer is here, present, ready. All we need do is reach out and grab the lifeline. All we need do is turn to God in our hearts. Once we are able to do this, our own voices will match that of this psalm. Once we accept and embrace this God who rescues, we will know the power and wonder of a grateful heart. We will then understand what it means to be saved and our impulse, our desire will be to "offer a thanksgiving of sacrifice as we call upon the name of the Lord."

Psalm 116:1-4, 12-19

If there's one thing that people universally appreciate, it's being heard. Nothing is quite as debilitating as talking and talking to someone and knowing down deep that the words are not penetrating; not being absorbed. Often, it's not the answer that people care about so much as knowing that their concerns were actually heard.

In this psalm, we hear this sentiment loud and clear. "I love the Lord," why? Because he "inclined his ear." In other words, because [he] listened! The catch here is that those who are calling upon God to listen sometimes mistake listening with agreement. As the old preacher said, "God always answers prayers. Sometimes [he] says, 'No.'" Yes, God listens. Indeed, God yearns for us to lean into the grace, acceptance, and forgiveness that are there for us. God hears and embraces all that we are as human creations. This, incredibly, is unconditional.

However, it is an adolescent faith that confuses God's listening with affirmation. Yes. God loves and accepts us but is definitely not willing to leave us as we are. God loves us unconditionally, but that doesn't mean that (he) is necessarily thrilled with our behavior. And it doesn't follow that those who believe will get the things for which they ask.

The call here comes to this. Beyond God's open ears comes a call for radical trust and obedience. No matter what the answer to prayer; no matter what fortune or misfortune may ride in on the dawn, the call comes for us to "offer a thanksgiving sacrifice" to God for the great abundance given. Now, those who are in the midst of grief and suffering might be tempted to say, "What abundance?" Those who, like Job, have been tested almost beyond endurance might be tempted to withhold their praise and thanksgiving until this God delivers.

But this temptation is to be resisted. Wherever life's journey finds us, God has already delivered. The gift of life, the miracle of breath and being, the jaw-dropping awe of realizing that there is one who created us and knows everything about us, and still through it all, loves us. This, finally, is what brings us to our knees and opens our mouth in praise. This, is the wonder and power that pulls us to the one who "inclines his ear to us."

Psalm 118:1-2, 14-24

It's Easter. For us, this is a day of new beginnings. It is the ultimate moment. Christ is risen! In the wake of Easter lilies, bunnies, and too, too much candy, a barrage of pat phrases echo above the Easter morning trumpets. "The shackles of death have been broken." "O death where is thy sting?" We have heard it before.

But what, really, does this mean for us? How does such a notion brush up against our everyday existence? Christ is risen. Well, good. The world continues much as before and little seems to have changed. Christ is risen, and how many people around the world died in a hail of bullets today or perished from hunger or grinding oppression?

Truly, what does it mean to say Christ is risen?

No short little essay can, of course, provide the definitive answer, but this psalm does provide us with a beginning. When we say, with the psalmist, that "the Lord is our strength and our might," we have said a mouthful.

The resurrection of Jesus Christ, you see, is no mere smoke and mirrors magic show designed to impress the impressionable. It is nothing short of a total rearrangement of life itself. In rising from the dead, Christ didn't just become the most powerful figure in our lives. He actually transformed power itself and redefined it for all time. Christ is risen, and the fundamental understanding of power in the world has been up-ended. The first shall now be last. Those who have been full will now go away empty. That which we have understood as powerful is now shown to be weak.

163

Take a piece of paper and draw a line down the middle. On the left side write down the things that our culture, or as Paul would say, "this world" considers as powerful. Guns, money, prestige, material possessions, all of it. On the other side we make a list of how God now defines and uses power in the risen Christ. Here we write words like "servanthood," "love," "forgiveness," "self-denial," and so forth.

If we look at these contrasting understandings of power or strength, it quickly becomes clear that as followers of Jesus Christ we are called to what amounts to a countercultural understanding of power.

This is the crux of what has happened in the resurrection of Jesus Christ. This is no mere revolution where Jesus comes and sits at the head of the table where someone else once sat. No, in rising from the dead, Jesus kicks over the table.

If "the Lord is our strength," then we will refuse to utilize the power of this world. If we trust in the "might of the Lord," then we will not trust in violence or any of the workings of this world's power mechanisms.

Indeed, Christ's rising changes everything. In the resurrection, God has literally created a new reality. All that is needed now is for his followers to reject the powers of this world and to live into that reality; live into the strength and might of the Lord.

Psalm 118:1-2, 14-24

Power is basic to our existence as human beings. How we define and utilize power determines much about how our lives and history move forward. Our history as a biblical people calls us to examine this carefully. Across the arc of our history we have had two choices, generally speaking, to make about power. The first is to choose to invest our hearts and energies in God's power. This choice is articulated by the psalmist here in verse 14. "The *Lord* is my strength and my might. He has become my salvation." The italics here are necessary because it is not a given that we choose God as the source of our power. The second option we have is to decide to wield power on our own. The classic story of this is found in 1 Samuel 8, where the people reject God in favor of a king so that the people can be like "other nations." It seems that keeping up with the Joneses is older than we thought.

The power wielded by us is what Paul refers to as the powers of "this world," or the cosmos. It is characterized by threats of force or coercion. It is enforced by rigid economic stratification and control, and it inevitably leaves a wake of death and injustice in its path.

Conversely, the power of God is defined and used quite differently. If we find power and strength in God, this power is underscored by adoration and love. It is carried out with justice and equity, and it insists on equity for all people. Following in the footsteps of this kind of power we find very different results (Isaiah 61).

On Easter Sunday we see this power burst forth from an empty tomb to conquer death itself. God's power comes to us as the ultimate redemptive act of self-giving love. In God's act in Christ, power is not merely given to another leader in a long line of despots. Power itself is transformed so that what we thought was strong is actually weak (1 Corinthians 1:18 ff). Those who are wise are now seen as foolish and the rich and powerful no longer hold sway.

Yes, God is our strength and our salvation. Out of the two choices we have to make regarding power in our lives, it seems clear which one we should make. Perhaps this Easter we will choose the risen one as our source of power and life, our hope and our redemption.

Psalm 118:1-2, 14-24

Today, Christian people everywhere celebrate an incredibly absurd notion. Through the cultural overlay of bunnies and chocolate is found the shocking assertion that death is not the end. In a world where death is treated as the final sanction, the ultimate finish, this crazy notion asserts itself once again.

Today there are "glad songs of victory" (v. 15) as an open-mouthed and amazed people stand at the door to an empty tomb. Today this group rises with shouts and gasps as the voice of the

165

holy says, "I shall not die, but I shall live!" (v. 17). Today we flaunt a world that wallows in death and insist that life wins in the end. Even though the "stone" was rejected by the builders of this world, we claim it now as the "cornerstone of a new reality."

In this psalm we see the seeds of a new reality planted, awaiting germination on this resurrection day. It is a new reality in which the definition and use of power have been completely up-ended. "Death," as we read in Revelation, "is no more." It is a reality where the "proud and mighty are scattered" (Luke 1:51), and where the first are now to be last. It is a reality where the dividing walls (Galatians 3:27) erected to keep people apart and alienated from one another have come down in an avalanche of love and compassion. It is a reality where the fear that is used to manipulate and manage is cast out by the "perfect love" (1 John 4:18) of this resurrected Lord.

It's Easter Sunday.

Today, an invitation has been issued to enter into this new reality as a community of faith. It is an invitation that comes with an RSVP. How is it that the church will respond? Will the faithful take the lilies, plant them in the backyard, and get on with business as usual? Will the church simply send back the card saying that we are unable to attend?

No. This new reality, this shining new life is "the Lord's doing," and the call comes to the church to embrace it anew. The call comes to the people gathered to rise up and say the closing words of this psalm with a slight twist. "This is the reality that God has made! Let us rejoice and be glad in it! Let us rejoice and choose to live together in it!"

Psalm 118:14-29

Anyone can throw a party. It's easy to jump up and down and shout loud "alleluias." Pay the DJ, set out the drinks and the buffet table, and that's about it. At first, it's a blast! Whirling bodies and pulsing rhythms fill the night. Laughter and clinking glasses seem like an endless and joyful dialogue. But, by midnight it all starts to get a little old. People get tired of shouting and dancing and head home because they have to work the next day. The DJ was only hired for a few hours and he, perhaps, has another gig at an after-hours club across town. The food is mostly gone, and there is a ghastly mess to clean up by the few people who weren't smart enough to leave earlier.

Yes. The party is easy. It's the next day that's hard.

The thrill of the resurrection and the empty tomb spill and disperse through another week at work only to find the faithful with the second part of this psalm. One can hear the stifled yawn and the whispered assertion, "Wasn't Easter last week?" "This sounds awfully familiar."

In truth, the Easter "reality," though thrilling at the start, is no easy thing to maintain. Thrust back into the sullen world as the people are, this Easter notion of new life and new beginnings; even of a new reality are kind of hard to hang onto when one's sales quota has been raised. If it's any comfort, it wasn't easy for the disciples, either.

There is, in this post-Easter haze, what poet and prophet, Daniel Berrigan, has referred to as a "smog of disbelief," even among the most passionate of believers. It is indeed difficult to keep celebrating the "day that the Lord has made," when the people live, work, and breathe in a world that the Lord has had little to do with — indeed a world the people are called to shun.

It is at this point that the incredible gift of community takes hold. Yes, each person who shouts, "Alleluia," on Easter Sunday has to step back into a Good Friday world. Yes, each person who claims the new reality in Jesus Christ must return to the reality of time clocks and quotas. But praise God! There is a Christian community that remembers the alleluias. Praise God there is a community where this new reality not only survives but thrives. Here, in the sanctuary of community the party continues. Perhaps the songs are different. Maybe the dance steps change, but the table is spread, the feast is always ready as people shout once more, "Blessed is he who comes in the name of the Lord!"

Psalm 119:97-104

A devotee of the writings of the apostle Paul might look at such a psalm as this and shake his head while making a clucking sound with their tongue. One can almost hear Paul's refutation of law even as love for that law is pronounced herein. But Paul's call for grace alone notwithstanding, the law is wonderful.

Martin Luther King Jr. once said that the law couldn't keep someone from hating him, but it could keep them from lynching him. Law has its place. God's law has its place as well. The Ten Commandments for example, remain pretty much intact in our civil law today, though one must admit that the adultery thing has kind of slipped. Still, though, we recognize almost universally the laws that forbid us to kill, steal, and even lie. Indeed, at this writing there is a government official looking at serious jail time because of telling lies about his actions.

The ability for the human community to come together and acknowledge some of the universal realities that make life livable really is quite remarkable. Imperfect, certainly, but still a thing of wonder. The law of the Lord is indeed a thing of beauty. It is not a club to be used to coerce, but rather something prayerful to meditate upon (v. 1) all the day long. The law puts furniture in the room of our humanity. It gives us something to sit upon. It decorates the halls and puts rails on the stairway.

Even the Lord's law, however, needs to change from time to time. Look at the Deuteronomic code. We have pretty much abandoned stoning people for adultery, and though we still decry it, most of us are glad the stones have been left on the street. Other laws, too, have changed. From slavery to dietetic laws, we have learned, with the old hymn "Once To Every Man And Nation," that "time makes ancient good uncouth."

God's law is like creation. It is organic, dynamic, changing, and fluid. We run into problems when we forget this and try to make the law into rigid, unchanging pillars. In fact, humans run into trouble when they try to resist change in general. Change is one of God's most basic laws. Change is built into all creation. It is part and parcel of all that exists. Yet, humans, in their insecurity and desire for a false sense of stability, try to resist it. From church to state to nature itself, we resist it. And yet it comes. Change is part of the ineffable will of God.

We come to the beauty of God's law. We arrive at the wonder of it all and come at last to a meditation on the changing immutability of an incredible God.

Psalm 119:105-112

A fond memory emerges of a young child attending church camp, walking darkened pathways each night from cabin to outhouse and back again. It was, for some inexplicable adolescent reason, completely unacceptable to use a flashlight. Only babies would use a light. So, each night this group of young men would stumble, fall, collide with trees and stumps all the way from sleeping cabin to outhouse and back again. It was a time of chuckles and giggles, a memory that is cherished.

Now as a middle-aged adult, the experience lives as a metaphor in the mind. Today, it seems as if the whole world is on its way to the outhouse in the dark. Benumbed and amused to death by the constant bombardment of media messages, we walk blithely along in the dark shadows of a consumer-obsessed pathway toward death. Whole nations head down particular pathways refusing to turn on the light to see where they might actually be going. And all the while the light is there — available. All that needs happen is a flip of the switch.

"Thy word is a lamp unto my feet."

Indeed, God's word is exactly the flashlight we need as we stumble through the eerie darkness of our lives. God's word as given us in holy scripture and God's word revealed to us in Jesus Christ all shed a wonderful light through the darkness in which most people walk.

This word gives the light of compassion and justice; the radiance of hope and new life. This word offers a chance to see, not just what is immediately in front of us on the path, but also to look on ahead. If we live in this light and walk by its brilliance we can see down the pathway to where the journey will take us. Living and walking by the light of God's word leads the people down the pathways of peace. It illuminates the way ahead and shows that it is the way of fairness and equity. Of course we may stumble at times. There will always be rocks and roots along the way.

It just needs to be said that it isn't necessary to strike out in the darkness anymore. It isn't necessary unless human community resembles a cadre of adolescent boys on their way to the outhouse with something to prove.

Psalm 119:137-144

Protestant Christians love to talk about grace. Spouting the words of Paul, many a preacher goes on and on about how "the Law" has fallen before the mighty wonder of God's grace in Christ Jesus. It's true. God's grace is sufficient for all. Yet still, God's "decrees," and "precepts," do matter. Even Jesus said he did not come to abolish the law, but to see it fulfilled (Matthew 5:17). Even though contemporary folk get a little itchy with rules and regulations, the truth is that even in the shadow of grace, rules are a pretty good idea.

The Ten Commandments (Exodus 20:1-17), of course, come readily to mind. These are not precepts that arise out of a puffed-up religiosity, but rather from the rock-bottom practicality of human existence. Stealing is prohibited because it's difficult to have any kind of human intercourse if we're constantly taking things from each other. It would behoove certain individuals and corporations to attend to this detail. Similarly, fidelity in marital relations is not simply a hollow moralism. It is a trust-building, relationship-deepening commitment that has many rewards and benefits — both personal and social. Those entering into such covenant relationships should consider this. Killing is prohibited because, once again, human enterprise — even its existence is threatened by it. And yes, it would be a good idea for governments to consider this. And in our workaholic-frenzied culture, the idea of one day a week for rest isn't such a bad idea, is it? Perhaps our employers might think about this.

Indeed, God's "law is truth." God's decrees are "righteous forever."

The problem isn't with the decrees; it's with those for whom the rules are made. God's decrees require God's grace, and too often this is forgotten. As Jesus wryly noted, "The sabbath is made for people, not people for the sabbath" (Matthew 2:27). While we esteem and lift up God's righteous law, it's important, even critical that we take Jesus' words to heart. The perfect law of God was made for us, to assist and guide. We were not made to be bent and formed around the law.

With this psalm, let the people celebrate God's wonderful precepts and decrees. Search throughout creation and cannon, claiming the power of God's law. And then, with humility and prayer, let these same people remember for whom the law was created.

Psalm 121

There is perhaps no better feeling than knowing that someone "has your back." Having someone's back is a term that arose from urban street fighting where a partner or ally would stay with you and protect your back in the thick of the fray. When someone has your back, you don't worry about being hit from behind. When someone has your back you can concentrate on the struggle in front of you without worrying about dangers you cannot see. When someone has your back you feel protected, secure, safe.

In God, the psalmist finds the king of all street fighters to have his back. His help doesn't merely come from a trusted compadre, it comes from the creator of the universe! "*My* help (emphasis on the word, "my") comes from the Lord!" The wonderful implication here is that the adversary can bring on all comers. God's on the scene. God's in charge now. No matter what comes, it can be handled.

The trick in all this, though, is trust.

Whether it's a buddy from the "hood," or the Lord God, letting someone come to your defense means you have to trust the source of the help. Think about it. Not trusting someone who has your back is pretty much the same as having two adversaries. So it is that these words come with a simple surety. Trust runs through the psalm like a drum keeping silent time. No doubt here. No wavering or wondering in this proclamation. God won't allow my foot to be moved even an inch. God doesn't slumber or sleep. God is on the job.

It would be an easy thing here to go the smoke and magic mirrors route, assuming that trusting in God is equivalent to some kind of insurance policy. It's the old *quid pro quo*. If I believe in God then thus and such will or won't take place. Not so. Life and death continue to flow forward bringing everything with it. Earthquakes, fires, wars, and disease will not take a holiday because of trust in God. What will evaporate, however, is the fear with which we confront life's challenges. What will come is a confidence and sense of power that emanates from the sure feeling that God's got your back. In truth, can it get any better than that?

Psalm 122

In this day of turmoil and violence in the Middle East, a call to "pray for the peace of Jerusalem," is a poignant one indeed. Originally said by pilgrims coming from across Israel to Jerusalem, this psalm today holds a broader and deeper significance.

As body counts rise and anger increases, it is a prayer worth repeating. May "peace be within your walls, and security within your towers." Certainly the Middle East is convulsing with violence, even as these words are written. But the peace of Jerusalem is also the peace of the world. This psalm resonates with voices that pray for peace throughout our world. Across the globe today there are wars virtually everywhere. Indeed, in the United States, the expenditure on arms is in the trillions of dollars. It is hard to have "security within our towers" when all the resources of the nation are squandered on military adventures. It is difficult to have peace within our own walls when we ourselves are not agents of peace.

By all means, let the people pray for the peace of Jerusalem. But the children's hymn of old comes back in haunting echoes. "Let there be peace on earth, and let it begin with me." Let there be peace on earth and let us call our own nation to account in its military spending and pre-emptive wars. Let there be peace on earth and let it begin with a nation who offers food, healing, and medicine rather than trade in arms and munitions. Let there be peace on earth, and let the voices of our citizens call for diplomacy and cooperation rather than threats and confrontation.

"For the sake of our friends and relatives," and for the sake of our sisters and brothers around the world, let this be the moment that people of faith commit to working for justice and for peace. Let this be the moment that prayers for peace become holy actions for peace. And, as the final words of this psalm indicate, let us seek the good of all, for the sake of the house of our God. For the sake of the planet created by God, for the sake of the many wonderful lands and cultures, let us look beyond ourselves and dedicate our lives to seeking the good of all.

As we prepare to welcome the Prince of Peace, can there be any other prayer? Can there be any other focus for our lives?

Psalm 123

A wise preacher once said that original sin did not involve an apple or a big snake. He said that original sin was really humanity's obsessive need to be in charge of things. He also added that after all these millennia, it could hardly be called "original." There is truth in these words. The despoiling of our planet is the result of our inability to discern the difference between stewardship and being in charge. The millions of people who suffer from the horrors of war are the result of people insisting that they are in charge. The grinding poverty that poisons the planet emerges from the notion that some people are in charge and have a right to more food and money than other people have. Who can do anything but throw up their hands in despair when they recount the struggles in church communities that come from people wanting to be ... in charge?

The preacher had it right. Human beings find it next to impossible to simply fall to their knees and offer themselves in submission to the one who is greater. Nothing is more healing than being able to give all our struggles and pain — all our brokenhearted yearnings and woes over to God. It is to this kind of submission that this beautiful psalm speaks.

Here, in a few verses, is a scene of glory. This isn't the glory of the battlefield or the victory ring of the stock market bell. This is God's glory. It is that moment of truth that somehow comes so rarely. On bended knee with eyes lifted upward, the need to control and be in charge is finally relinquished in this prayer for mercy. All pretense has been dropped. All bets are off. Now the power arrangement is understood; embraced. Like a servant waiting for the master or a maid waiting for her mistress, this person waits now for God.

The almost-comic part of it all is that an integral part of our human control issue is that we hate waiting. Whether it's supermarket checkout lines or the harvest of seasonal fruit, we simply do not like to wait. Yet wait we must.

On our knees, having given all to God, we submit finally to God's timing and wait on God's mercy. This is the beginning of wisdom. This is the edge of salvation.

Psalm 124

The words to this psalm bring to mind the phrase imprinted on a huge monument to Germany's fallen in World War I. Located outside Leipzig in the former East Germany, this towering pile of stones has inscribed on it in huge letters, *"Gott mit uns!"* In English, this can be translated into "God is on our side." In that same struggle, the forces allied against Germany also thought that God was on their side. It is a bit of a problem. For eons, people across the globe have tried to press God into service in their wars and struggles. One can only wonder whether God simply shook a cosmic head and wept over the slaughter.

History's list of those who counted God as ally is indeed long. However, we in the line of Judeo-Christian heritage have carved out a rather large footing in this arena. Indeed, much of our early heritage is rooted in an identity as ones who are chosen by God. There really is little sense in trying to deny this. It is our story.

We were lifted up by God and rescued from slavery in Egypt. God parted the waters for our ancestors and used those same waters to destroy Pharaoh's army. Our story takes us through the wilderness and into Canaan where God assisted in the victory to gain the land. Beyond this, there are numerous stories of God's special favor for the people of Israel.

All this really begs for the big question. What happens when both sides claim God as ally? How does God choose sides? Or to put it more succinctly: Does God choose sides — especially in war?

There is one story attributed to Mark Twain. It is perhaps myth, but the point remains cogent. Mark Twain, in referring to the Spanish-American War, commented that it is not whether God is on our side, but whether we are on God's side. It is a question that should be asked often. God is on the side of the poor and the oppressed. Are we on our God's side? God is on the side of justice and hope. Are we on God's side? God is on the side of new life and forgiveness. Are we on God's side?

Psalm 124

Everyone needs someone who is on their side. This is not about friendship, though that's important. It's not about lovers and spouses, though life would be pretty drab without them. This is not a mere trifle of a need. It is about survival. Everyone requires an ally, a supporter, someone who will be a "rear guard" (Isaiah 58:8). Whether it's bullies on the school yard or a friend or mentor to walk with you, we need people who will help us. Without such support, life becomes literally impossible. In short, we cannot make it alone. In the trials and struggles of our lives we need each other.

We also need, as our psalm indicates, to have God on our side. After all, if you're in a fight for your life, wouldn't God be a bit helpful? Wouldn't you be saying with the psalmist, "If it had not been the Lord who had been on our side..."?

This, however, has proven to be a dangerous assertion. How many corpses have been piled up by soldiers justifying their actions because God was on their side? Today, as extremism from many faiths claims lives with the assumption that God is on their side, this is an important thing to consider.

It's safe to say that God is indeed on our side. God created us and loves us. God knows us and calls us by name. God yearns over us and beckons us into lives of faithfulness. God even sent the Son to die for us. If that doesn't show us that God's on our side, nothing does.

But God is not on our side no matter what we do. God does not stand and cheer as innocent people are slaughtered in bomb attacks, whether they are suicide bombers, or bombers in fighter jets. God is not on the side of oppressors or war makers. God is not on the side of anyone who "hits with a wicked fist" (Isaiah 58:4), or exploits the poor. God is not a puppet available for us to trot out in justification for what *we* would like to do. Indeed, it is the reverse which is true. God's voice comes to us calling us to do God's will, and not our own.

Many who have experienced God's saving action in their lives can identify with this psalm. It is powerful. Yet a word of caution posed as a query: Could it be that the question really isn't whether God's on our side, but rather if we are on God's side?

Psalm 125

Trusting in God is the most challenging and basic element of faith. It is the foundation upon which everything else rests. It is the very core around which everything else is arranged. This trust, though, is harder than generally advertised. Moreover, it is not a task that is achieved or a project that gets completed. Trusting God is a lifelong struggle for every person of faith. The trusting ones may be, as the psalm tells us, as unmovable as mountains. But that doesn't mean that trust comes easily.

The thing about trusting God is that it means that we automatically do not, then, trust in other things. If we place our trust in God, it is absolute. We do not trust in economic systems or governments, we trust in God. We do not trust in culture or social norms, we trust in God. Perhaps most difficult is the reality that we dare not trust in our own efforts and machinations. We trust in God and God alone.

This is a tall order. It puts one in sympathy with the rich young ruler in the gospel of Matthew (19:25). If this is the deal, "Who then can be saved?" Actually trusting in God puts us out of step with the world in which we live. It calls us out of structures, out of prevailing attitudes, and into a context of grace. Yes, it's hard to do.

Partly because this is so difficult, the culture of church has managed to reduce faith to a list of doctrinal dictates. All one needs to do is nod in assent to these articles and poof! You're a believer. Belief, however, is not a mere assent to a list of biblically dubious propositions. It is about trusting in God. Indeed, the English word for "belief" in much of Christian scripture is actually the Greek word, *pistus*, which means trust.

The church's understanding of belief is largely a ruse. It is a pantomime of faith calling us to mutely act out doctrines and to trust in them rather than in God. Such doctrines and institutional trappings are only appropriate if they lead to trust in God. This is what Jesus meant when he said that the sabbath was made to serve us. We were not made to serve the sabbath (Mark 2:27).

Yes, the trusting God stuff is not easy. But it is a source of joy. When we manage to let go of our egos and our need to be in charge, when we give it all to God, the sense of joy that emerges is amazing. When we can devote our energies and passions, not to our wants and needs, but to God's, there is a freedom that is nearly indescribable. Paul tries to get at it in Romans 8:21, where he refers to this as the "freedom of the glory of the children of God."

If the church could lean into this kind of trust, revival and church growth would not be an issue. If Christians could leave behind their ideology-laden agendas and trust in God, divisions would cease. If each of us, each day could reach for this kind of trust, what a world we could build. What a world we could build.

Psalm 126

Some dreams feel so real that waking is a moment of profound confusion; a shudder of dislocation. The first part of this psalm is just such a dream. A memory of times gone by, times of good fortune and joy. But the writer awakes to the bitter pill of reality with a mournful cry.

That was then. This is now.

How often do we live in dreams of times gone by? The hard answer is, "Too often." How many members of how many declining churches sit at coffee hour sharing the way things used to be in the good old days? "I remember when the church was full!" "Back then, of course, we had 600 members!" "Those were the days." And, of course, there are the famous seven last words of the church. "We never did it that way before!"

While Israel may have comforted itself with memories of the return from Babylon, we can draw no such comfort. We do not have the luxury of living in the wavy mirage of a past whose memory is blurred by good intentions. No, we are the church of Jesus Christ on the edge — once again — of Christmastime. We look toward a Messiah who comes while we are waist deep in denial. We, too, long for days gone by. We, too, remember a day when our "mouths were filled with laughter" and "tongues with shouts of joy."

The vision to which we are called in this time is not a throwback to distant histories. It's not a desperate rush to preserve what little seems left of the old ways. The vision to which we are called in these days can be found as we embrace the reversals that the psalmist shares.

Our Advent vision harmonizes with Mary who sings of a God who brings down the powerful and lifts up the lowly, a God who makes certain that those who have "sown in tears will reap with shouts of joy."

This is not a vision rooted in the past, but a dream of what is possible with the power of God's love with us. Now we can awaken from distant reveries and place our feet on the ground of reality. Now we can reach together to a future filled with hope and new beginnings. Now we can build in places of devastation. Whether it be our own cities, or our own hearts; whether it be the rubble of distant battlefields or the wasteland of our benumbed spirits, we can build anew. The harvest is ready. It is time for us to "come home with shouts of joy, carrying the sheaves."

Psalm 126

Thanksgiving is a favorite holiday. There is nothing quite like this time when friends and families gather for a feast and a time of thankfulness. It truly is a great holiday on the calendar. However, it's important for us to realize that in the mix of our lives, Thanksgiving is not a Christian holiday. Thanksgiving was formally declared a holiday by President Lincoln during the struggles of our Civil War. In the ensuing years, it has woven itself into our culture to such a degree that we mark it on our liturgical calendars as though it were part of our Christian calendar.

Only the severest of cynics would attack Thanksgiving as a holiday. After all, what could possibly be wrong with giving thanks? Nothing. Nothing is wrong with this holiday. Indeed, this writer spends a good portion of the months prior to Thanksgiving scouring cookbooks for new ways to stuff a turkey. No. Whatever you do, leave Thanksgiving alone.

The only point that needs to be made for us, as people of God, is that for us Thanksgiving is not a holiday. Let's continue to take that fourth Thursday in November as a time to give thanks and gather in warmth and love, but let's move forward and take it a step further as a people of faith. Let us embrace Thanksgiving, not as one day on the calendar, but as a way of being.

The Lord has indeed "done great things for us," and as we awaken to the many blessings God has given us, thankfulness is a natural response. The challenge to us, though, is to claim thankfulness as a way of life. The call to us is to awaken each morning with a thankful heart for the gifts of breath and life. The pathway open to us is the intentional shaping of our moments and days so that each breath, each step, each word spoken is an utterance of profound thanksgiving.

And it's this intentionality that is most difficult. We have a way of forgetting, of slipping away from what some church folk call "an attitude of gratitude." Yet the call to live our lives on purpose in the Lord continues to come to us, steadily, patiently, persistently.

On this Thanksgiving Day, then, perhaps the church can hear the call to be a people who live lives of thankfulness. Maybe your congregation could step into a renewal space, taking each moment

179

as an opportunity for thankfulness. Imagine, on this day of thanks, what would happen if every person entered each new experience, even the challenging ones, as a new chance to give thanks to God for the innumerable blessings that have been bestowed upon us.

Psalm 126

There's nothing quite as wonderful as looking at an old car that's been restored to its former luster. A 1932 Ford Victoria Coupe, rumbling down the road brings a thrill. The rust has been cleaned off, the torn upholstery replaced, and missing windows have been installed. It is a work of art. It is also a work of love. Such restoration projects, as anyone involved in them can attest, are not for the weak of heart. Restoring a classic automobile requires painstaking attention to detail and the patience of Job. After the body has been sanded and repaired, layer after layer of paint must be applied and rubbed down. Then comes polish and more rubbing. Engines, too, need to be rebuilt. Sometimes needed parts aren't available and have to be custom made. This is quite a job indeed!

As the Lenten season draws to a close, we look, as a people, to a time when God will restore our fortunes. Unlike the people in this psalm, however, we don't look to the restoration of a nation, or even of the car we're driving. We look to restoration through new life in Jesus Christ.

Still, though, the question of restoration bears asking. As we look to the restorer of all things to attend to us, what is it that requires fixing or repair? What is it that might need to be replaced? For some, it might be a broken heart. Others might be steeped in anger and find themselves in need of scraping off the rust of resentment. Still others might find the need for a new engine; a new driving purpose. In the pastor business this is called "burn-out." How does God restore a worn out people — a broken-down church — a deflated and over-used pastor?

There are, of course, many answers. One, though, that this psalm touches on is the ability to dream (v. 1). When God restored the fortunes, the people were like ones who dreamed. One needs ask, though, which came first — the chicken or the egg? The dream or the restoration?

The ability to dream, to vision, to see a new reality is the beginning of a holy process. It is the ability to see that pile of rust and rot and envision a gleaming Model A in pristine shape. God sees us that way and envisions a new life, a new beginning for us. The trick is for us to catch that vision; for God's people to grow vulnerable to seeing things a new way — a different way. God plants the dream seed in each heart. God envisions restoration and new life. God leads the way, then as now, into Jerusalem, to Gesthemane and Golgotha, and on to an empty tomb. Again, the trick is to catch the vision.

Psalm 127

There is a story about a pastor who worked for years to revive and grow a failing downtown church. After endless hours of work and effort, the church actually did begin to come to life. New members came, new ministries were born, and it seemed as if a miracle were taking place. Then the pastor was called to a new congregation. In a few years, after a succession of failed pastorates, the church closed. The pastor who had given so much of himself was devastated. It seemed that his work was "in vain."

Many people in our faith communities could relate stories from their lives about efforts they have made that have felt as though they were made for no purpose or no visible effect. In the folds of these stories lay wounded hearts and burned-out spirits. In the telling of these tales, we feel the exhaustion and frustration and sometimes the resignation of those who have had enough.

It is into such difficulties that the words of this psalm come. How often do we plan, work, and strive to get things accomplished, relying only upon our efforts and our will? How often do we fail to place the results of our work in God's hands? How often do we fail to trust in God's "all sufficient grace" (2 Corinthians 12:9) as we labor for what we believe to be God's work?

The words seem jarring, but they ring true. "Unless God builds the house, those who build it labor in vain." Unless we place our whole trust in God's grace and love, the chances are that we are "laboring in vain." The interesting thing in all this is that success and effectiveness are really not the point. The psalm doesn't say that if we trust in God we will meet with success. This is a false promise delivered far too often by those in ministry. What the promise of God's grace does offer is the reality that our labors, if they are rooted in trust in God, will not be in vain.

There is no guarantee about how things will turn out in the end. But if our work is rooted in God's love and grace, it will not be wasted. The church in our story may have closed, but the fact that lives were touched, hearts healed, and people brought to Christ cannot be altered. The labor of the years, though not resulting in the pastor's desire for a revitalized and growing church, was not in vain.

The psalmist reminds us, no matter where we labor, we must place the results and the trust in God. Then we can be freed to work hard, to give deeply of time and heart energy, knowing that the labor will not be in vain.

Psalm 130

Forgiveness is a concept common to most everyone. It covers a vast landscape, to be sure. In biblical understanding it is especially broad, linking together economic, social, divine, and interpersonal realities. Indeed, it is pervasive and foundational to Judeo-Christian faith. However, in our contemporary world we cling with worn fingernails to forgiveness as a sparse, seldom-used interpersonal notion. If utilized, it comes when two people have a quarrel, and one *forgives* the other — simple — clean — easy — not too intrusive.

Yet, for people of faith, this cannot be the case. Forgiveness is the ground upon which we walk. It is the air we breathe and the eyes through which we see. It is integral, not only to our self-understanding but to our apprehension of God. Forgiveness is not just the stock and trade of faith, it has to do with the fiber of human reality.

Human beings need forgiveness. We need it because we are broken, flawed, and frail. We need it because, as the middle schooler in church wryly comments, "We mess up a lot." The words of this psalm go directly to this point.

With a full and painful awareness of culpability and responsibility the writer comes clean. If God kept score, none of us could stand (v. 4). How true it is.

But with God, there is forgiveness. Not a trite burying of the hatchet, not a sweeping under the rug of past hurts and insults, and not the strained fabric of denial, but true and miraculous forgiveness. For this, the soul will "wait." For this, the spirit dares to "hope."

True forgiveness changes things. It wipes clean the slate of anger and hurt. It breathes fresh air onto old wounds so that they can heal. It lifts the burden of guilt and allows for new beginnings. Yet, such powerful new possibilities are seldom realized in the wake of a narrow and self-absorbed notion of forgiveness.

Perhaps a fresh reading of this psalm can expand our understanding of forgiveness to include each and every aspect of the lives we lead together. Maybe if each person stopped to "wait" upon God's grace and forgiveness, a whole world of new opportunities might present themselves. Imagine what would happen in this nation if the idea of forgiveness reached into the economic realm? Forgiveness of debts in a debt-ridden world? It would be nothing short of revolutionary.

Picture, too, a world where the great social sins were answered, not with even greater sins, but forgiveness. We need only look to the Truth and Justice Commission of South Africa to see that such a thing can happen. Finally, it stirs the soul to conjure up a world where interpersonal relationships were marked with the practice of a true and transformational forgiveness.

There is indeed forgiveness with you, O Lord! And while we wait, let us dare to practice this divine art across the spectrum of our lives.

Psalm 130

"Patience," the old ditty goes, "is a grace, and Grace is a little girl who doesn't wash her face." There is, it would seem, more truth to the rhyme than first occurs to one loosing it flippantly from the tongue. Patience is indeed a grace. It is a gift, a charism, if you will, which is not found in great supply these days.

Waiting patiently for anything is a challenge. Whether it's in the supermarket line or sitting still on the freeway, we don't much like waiting. We want what we want, and we want it now! Wait? No thanks. I'll just go someplace else. These situations can be tough enough, but what happens when we must wait for God?

When a relationship shatters and we are broken and alone, how do we wait for God? When illness takes us and we are but a shadow of what we remember ourselves to be, how is it that we wait for God? What happens when justice fails or evil triumphs? What can be done when a nation drifts slowly but most certainly into the maw of religious travesty while torture and maltreatment of the poor become business as usual? How, when powerlessness sweeps over us like storm-driven surf, do we wait for God?

The answer is simpler than one might think. We cry. This is not the whining cry of a child who doesn't get what he or she wants. It is wailing that emerges from deep within the soul. "Out of the depths," we cry to God.

Some would say that this does no good. But life would beg to differ. After a good cry, we do feel better. After a gut-wrenching session of keening, our bellies are emptied out, and a kind of calm envelops us. Even the medical community will tell us that our tears serve to carry toxins out of our systems. So it seems that crying out does help after all.

Then, when the crying's done; when we are spent and calm, we can practice the gift of patience as we await God to come in God's time, not our own. And in the waiting, hope is born. In the waiting, we surrender our egos and our agenda. In the waiting, we give ourselves to something far beyond our ability to comprehend. In the waiting, we give ourselves to God.

Psalm 130

Back in the '60s, there was a phenomenon known as trading stamps. At grocery stores and other vendors, shoppers would receive an amount of stamps proportionate to their spending. The idea was that you would save these stamps in little books conveniently provided by the stores and then turn them in for all kinds of delectable prizes.

So, with books brimming with stamps, people would go to what was known as a redemption center. There would be gleaming products on the shelves and smiling attendants to help. You could turn your stamps in at this redemption center for an electric frying pan, a fancy new steam iron, or a backyard barbecue grill.

All in all, it was a neat arrangement and a very clever marketing ploy. The closest thing to it today are the airlines who offer frequent flyer miles that can be redeemed, after you accumulate enough, for free flights.

This sense of redemption is the coinage of our culture. Like a flat stone hurled against the surface of the water, it skims and skips along without that satisfying plunk of a splash. For us, redemption is a kind of barter. We redeem our stamps or our miles for goods and services that we desire. After all, they were called "trading" stamps, right?

But for Israel, and other nations in the long line of history, redemption is a somewhat different matter. This kind of redemption is no mere visit to the trading post. This kind of redemption has to do with being rescued. In this psalm, the writer howls out from the depths of misery and begs for God's redemption.

Thinking about those trading stamp redemption centers, one wonders about how our churches fare in this regard. Would we call our churches redemption centers? Do we engage in worship and ministry with the notion of redemption in mind? And if so, what does it look like? Do we invite people to trade in their "iniquities" (v. 3) for God's saving power? If so, what does *that* look like? Are we able to move beyond the trading stamp model of redemption and go deeper into the notion that we are all in need of rescuing, and that we are all called to "wait" upon God's salvation?

It is a tension that comes to us all as we strive to be faithful. How is it that we wait upon our redemption? How is it that we teach and lead? How is it that we build communities that are redemption centers?

Psalm 131

Humility is at the core of faith. Nice statement, that. But what does it mean? Most assume that good humble Christians stay in their places and don't disturb the waters of the world in which they live. In the larger culture, humility means staying out of the way and keeping one's mouth closed — be humble and be quiet.

This may be the view of the culture, or as Saint Paul would call it, "this world" (1 Corinthians 1:20), but it is not a biblical humility. Biblical humility is all about surrendering oneself to God. It has to do with laying down the narrow desires and wants of our own hearts so that God's desires can become our own. It has to do with laying down the ego so that the striving and accomplishments that drive us in this world can be given up in favor of God sitting in our driver's seat.

A humble Christian is not necessarily quiet. A spirit given over to God and God's way in the world might well become a strident voice for God. Martin Luther King Jr. was humble in that he accepted God's call and moved forward even though it put him and his family at risk. He was not quiet, but his soul was calm. He was not overly ambitious, but he had work to do. He was not occupied with "things too marvelous" for him. He was just pursuing God's call to justice.

A humble Christian is not necessarily without passion. Someone who has released spiritual baggage in their lives and claimed the power of God's Spirit can be singed with the flame of holy passion. Cesar Chavez burned with a passion for justice that comes from a depth of faith as he fought for the rights of migrant workers. Daniel Berrigan lit the fires of Pentecostal passion when he and brother, Philip, burned draft records in Catonsville, Maryland, during the Vietnam War. These are humble Christians.

Christian humility, it turns out, is anything but quiet or passive. It is, however, a soul at rest because it is has given all worldly concerns over to God. Ego, achievement, acquisition, approval of the world; all surrendered in order to more perfectly follow the holy one, in whom we find our hope and our salvation.

Psalm 132:1-12 (13-18)

The scholars tell us that this psalm was likely a liturgical piece used in the celebration of the Lord's enthronement. This, more than many other psalms, tells a story. From the finding of the ark in Ephrata (v. 6) onward, the story is told with power and passion. As a people who are rooted in story, it is important for us to look deeply at what is going on here. This is not merely a historic document dating likely to pre-exile times. Some scholars think it might be "deutoronomic." It, like all of holy scripture, has a message to offer us in the here and now.

Of the many ways we have of seeking and uttering that message, one way is to try and locate oneself within the story. That is, to read and pray deeply about the unfolding drama of this psalm and to see what it feels like to locate ourselves therein. What, for example, would it have felt like to be one of those who actually found the ark in Ephrata? Discovering the holy like that must have its own set of feelings and emotions, observations and conclusions. Then it would behoove us to consider where in life today are we discovering the holy? Is it found in the expected places? Is it uncovered on the way to something else? And if the holy is not being discovered today, why is that?

Or perhaps the role of the priests "clothed in righteousness" (v. 9) ought to be examined. What of today's clergy? What does it mean for a pastor serving in the twenty-first century to be "clothed with righteousness"? Does it speak to ethics? To prophetic witness? Does it go to the ways that pastors live — or not — as role models and witnesses for a congregation?

In the same verse, it might be powerful to examine the "saints" who are shouting for joy. Assuming with Saint Paul that "saints" is another word for the regular folk in the pews, one has to ask about the joy quotient. On a scale of one to ten, how joyful are the saints in our churches? This doesn't refer to contentment or placidity. It doesn't lead into happiness or good attendance. This is joy: deep, spirit-born joy. And, of course, the question immediately follows about the connection between the "priests clothed in righteousness" and the "saints" shouting for joy.

There are numerous places in this psalm for each person to find a location. There are equally numerous challenges lifted for us as we go forward to find ourselves in the sacred story.

Psalm 133

"How very good and pleasant it is when kindred live together in unity!" The words that open this powerful psalm are nearly universal in their ability to inspire. However, the dream somehow seems to rarely find itself materialized in our common life. Our nation is polarized to the point of being paralyzed. Our churches are at war among themselves, striking out at one another in internecine struggle. And globally, we are descending into a frenzy of greed and intolerance.

Where, one has to ask, is this unity?

Is unity to be found in common ideology or theology? Is it to be discovered in cultural homogeneity? The answer to each of these is a resounding, "No." Unity, if it is ever to be discovered and strengthened, is relational in nature. It is based, not in agreement over ideas or principles, but on the intimate knowledge and experience of human interaction.

To put this concept in the language of faith, we would say that our unity is in Jesus Christ. We, as the body of Christ, are in relationship through Christ. It is there and only there that we claim any hope for unity.

It is indeed good when this unity emerges. It is a unity not forged in conformity, but in the cauldron of human interaction. It is deeper than the inevitable conflicts that arise; broader than the countless perspectives we bring to the tables, and more powerful than forces that seek to divide and fracture.

Such unity as this is what our psalm attempts to describe. Like precious oil or morning dew, this unity is indeed precious. Like anything important or precious, this kind of unity requires intention, care, and constant effort. A good starting place for this effort is within our local congregations. How are we handling our relationships at church? Is the sanctity of relationships within Christian community a priority? Is there an intentional focus on helping people to feel safe and loved? Are there avenues for conversation, sharing, and prayer?

The world is starving for this kind of unity. Amid the chatter and panic of the media, perhaps this church can quietly and steadily begin to build a new vision and hope for the world. And just maybe, as it builds a unity based on relationships with one another and with Jesus Christ, there will be a chance for healing.

Psalm 133

Living in unity is a beatific vision. How wonderful it would be in our nation if, rather than vitriolic polarization, we would have unity. It would, as this psalm suggests, be "like the precious oil running down on the beard of Aaron." Imagine a day when national security is understood to be the result of building unity across the face of the globe, rather than hoarding the world's resources and maintaining a military force powerful enough to maintain our riches.

Focus the lens down now, closer to home. Dream a dream, if you can, of communities no longer divided by race or economic standing. Give birth in your heart to a new sense of unity. Sing a song of a unity that is not forged in stamped-out conformity, but rather, a unity that is woven of the tapestry of our God-given differences. This is a coming together rooted in the conviction that each person, and that truly means everyone, is created in the image of God.

The unity called for in this psalm is not this former kind of unity. It is a shalom unity. A holistic coming together that draws upon the strengths of all and makes secure the weaknesses of each person, community, or nation. This unity is nothing less than the kingdom of God. The building of such a unity is perhaps the primary calling from our God.

Here we are given a vision of its beauty. It is like the "dew of Hermon," a pastiche of a mist-shrouded morning in a pastoral setting. It is an ideal that is often brushed off as unattainable and seldom, if ever, strived for by us or any previous generation.

Unity is a blessing "ordained by God." It is, therefore, something that each pastor and congregation, each community across the nation ought to strive to achieve. Take a moment. Close the eyes. Still the heart. Allow a vision of a first step to God's unity in the community. Don't think big. Think of something that is "doable." One idea might be a "community partners" ministry, reaching out to those in the community that the church doesn't connect with at this time. Another effort might be a tutorial ministry that offers homework help with positive adult role models for children in your community that need both the help and the positive input.

Unity comes, not with a noble pronouncement, but with small steps such as these, taken prayerfully, and hearts full of God's love. Truthfully now, prayerfully, what steps can you take? When will you take them?

Psalm 137

This most poignant of psalms escapes as a cry from a people in exile. "How can we sing the Lord's song in a foreign land?" Violated, defeated, uprooted, and brought into slavery in a strange country, a people are further humiliated as their captors try to get them to sing one of the songs from their vanquished land. It's a joke. The tormentors "asked for mirth, saying, 'sing us one of the songs of Zion!' " Go ahead, use your strange instruments, show us your weird music!

It is this response that shows power. It is the spine of a people who ultimately cannot be defeated, who answer with a simple, "No." No. We will not sing for you. Indeed, how can we sing in this strange place? It is in the shelter of this "No" that a people, even in captivity, can stay free.

The power of "No," is universal. We see it in young children learning to navigate their world as they discover that they can refuse that spoonful of mashed peas. They can't articulate it perhaps, but the statement goes something like this: Hey! I am an individual. I am free. I can choose. I will not let you put that awful stuff in my mouth! No! More significant, perhaps, than a childhood refusal to eat, are other things to which we may or may not say, "No."

Saying "No" to hatred and greed has true and incredible power. Saying "No" to unjust laws sets the stage for positive change and growth. During the Civil Rights Movement, it was the simple "No" of Rosa Parks that sparked a revolution. "No. I will not move to the back of the bus." "No. I will not accept your attempts to enslave me."

Where, in the landscape of our lives do we need to say "No"?

Where in our personal lives does our "No" keep us free and maintain our integrity? In instances where we are expected to go along with something we know is wrong? Say, "No." At times when we observe injustice? Say, "No." What can be done when the resources of the community are used to hurt and harm others? Say, "No."

Yes, it's true. Always saying "No," can make one seem kind of negative. But remember, "No" is a multi-dimensional response. Pick it up. Turn it around. Look on the other side of "No," and you'll see. A "No" to war is a "Yes" to peace. A "No" to oppression in the workplace, is a "Yes" to justice and safety. A "No" to discrimination is a "Yes" to dignity.

So pick up your "No" and use it where needed. Don't be afraid to say it. Don't be afraid to use your body to articulate it. For in this "No" was not just the integrity of a long ago people in exile, it is also the location of our own.

Psalm 138

Few people write thank-you notes anymore. A word of thanks may be offered briefly when a gift is received or a favor done, but the custom of a formal written thank you has, for the most part, faded from our common life. It is a loss felt more deeply than conscience might admit. Not only has a civilized habit disappeared from our social horizon, but with it has gone an intentional sense of thankfulness. Social critics might label this as the result of a burgeoning sense of entitlement in an over-privileged generation. Perhaps this is so. But the purpose here is not social commentary so much as it is a call to thankfulness as an intentional ongoing way of living.

Psalm 138 evokes this sense of intentional and ongoing thankfulness. Here thanks are offered with the completeness of a "whole heart." Thanks come even though the writer walks through the "midst of trouble." Thanks go up every day and in every way to this God who accompanies, this God who is present, this God who delivers on his promises.

The thankfulness alluded to here is not merely a serial list of thanks for favors done or prayers answered. It bespeaks an attitude of thanksgiving. No matter what's happening or what state of life the writer experiences, the thanks keep coming. And it is here that a sense of invitation comes.

The reader is invited to this life of thankfulness along with the psalmist. The band strikes up a chord and the conductor is pointing directly at us. It's time for each person to take stock of the mighty doings of our God and to enter into an ongoing and constant state of thankfulness wherein our whole hearts are engaged in thanking God.

Each morning as the alarm clock sounds, give thanks for the gift of life and breath. Each hour as one more person is encountered, give thanks for the gift of human touch and contact. As each bite of food is consumed, be thankful for nourishment and the privilege of taste. Again, it is not so much remembering to say thank you each time as it is adopting thanksgiving as part of the process of thinking and feeling.

The invitation comes with gold engraving — join in a life of thanks and praise to this incredible God. It is a life well worth the living.

Psalm 139:1-6, 13-18

There's something about someone who knows you really well. It is a state of grace that slices across all other interactions. Sit across the table from a spouse of twenty years, a best friend of half a century, a sister or brother who has grown with you through the victories and the defeats. It's an amazing moment to look into the eyes of such a person and know ... that they know.

With a person like this all bets are off, all delusions and pretexts are washed away. The little lies we tell ourselves and the bigger ones we broadcast to others melt away across a table like this. For some, such vulnerability is terrifying. How does the old saying go? Once wounded, twice wary? Such fear is understandable. But the untold reality is that the fear wounds more deeply than that which causes it. The truth is that such vulnerability is the key to a liberation like no other.

When you are known completely, the constant grinding and wearing effort to be what we are not suddenly seems silly. When we are completely known, there is no cause for fear — no reason to hide. When we are known completely, we are free to be who we really are.

Spouses, siblings, and friends may be a part of the equation in all this, but God knows it all. Across the table from the holy, there is nothing hidden or kept secret. As the psalm says so powerfully, God knows when we sit down or stand up. God knows our thoughts and our thinking. Even the words we speak are known before they slip from our lips.

The thing that is almost "too wonderful" to comprehend is that knowing all this, God loves us still. In our weakness and our frailty, God loves us. In our bluster and our bravado, God loves us. In our seemingly limitless capacity for self-delusion, God loves us. God loves us as we are. Whether we sally forth, protected with our much-vaunted sense of self, or step into the storm stripped clean and vulnerable, God sees, knows, understands ... and loves.

This God with us, this God who knows us, this Emmanuel is hard to comprehend sometimes. The thoughts, as the psalmist notes, are "too weighty" for us. They are more numerous and vast than the sand. Yet, in it all, this God stays with us and goes the distance for us.

To quote an old Gershwin song that waxes eloquently about "plenty o' nuthin'," we have to ask the question, "Who could ask for anything more?"

Psalm 139:1-6, 13-18

One of the marvelous things about a long and happy marriage is that the partners really come to know one another. Being known is a precious gift. It is a reality that slices through all the pretense and machinations that occupy so much of our time and energy. When a husband starts to protest over something patently ridiculous, a sidelong, knowing glance creates silence because he knows that she knows. When a wife starts to overreact to something, a quiet hand on the shoulder brings calm because she knows that he knows. It's wonderful to be known. It's even more wonderful to be known and continue to be loved.

However, as close as two people might become in a committed relationship, there are still quiet, secret places. One is never completely known except by God. God knows it all. Before any pretense or cover-up is even imagined, God is already shaking a celestial head at our buffoonery. The psalm really says it all. Sleeping or waking, wherever we go, whatever we say, God knows us so thoroughly that all silly attempts at hiding or presenting some imagined sense of self are futile.

Then the psalmist really puts a finger on it. "Such knowledge is too wonderful for me...." There it is. The beauty of being known. And, just like a loving spouse, this God knows it all, every wart, misdeed, malfeasance, and reckless mistake, and loves you still. One wonders how deeply this gets factored into our spiritual practices. When we pray, God knows already what we will ask and why. When we go the church council to try to get something going, God knows our motives. Even those things we tell no one — God knows.

Do we interact with God with this assumption in place? In prayer, do we come knowing that God knows? In our daily walk as women and men of faith, do we consider that God knows? More than that, do we approach this God, knowing that God knows, and that even in the knowing loves us still so deeply that he gave himself for us? This is a love beyond imagining. Yet here it is, lavished upon us in the form of loving grace. To be known and loved like this. "It's too wonderful for me."

Psalm 139:1-12, 23-24

The definition of a true friend is someone who knows all there is to know about you and still loves you. More than that, a true friend is always there for you. In the modern vernacular, a true friend, knowing all there is to know about you, still "has your back." Most people present a careful construct of themselves to the world. Most people maintain a trove of secrets unknown, they think, to anyone but themselves. But a true friend knows and won't go away.

This is the kind of fealty we find in the description of God in this psalm. No matter where this writer goes, God is there. God discerns every thought, knows every action, and is aware of our vast capacity for self-delusion and untruth. God has a file on us that goes way back. God knows it all and, incredibly, still loves us utterly and completely.

This is nothing short of amazing. It is, in fact, almost too much to bear. So, with Jonah and a host of notable others, we try to flee. Like the psalmist, we choose a dizzying array of hiding places. Careers, drugs, sex, alcohol, serial relationships; the list is long, and through it all God is still there.

To accept a love this complete has to have ramifications. To accept a love like this means that we ourselves must abandon our carefully constructed sense of self. We must step back from our delusions of independence and power. We must lay down every ridiculous assumption and face God simply, truly, as we are. Then and only then can this unqualified and abundant love flow into our being and claim us. And most of us just don't want to go there. It is, or at least we believe it is, easier to stay put. "Better the devil you know ..." or something like that.

This true friend, however, stays faithful. God continues to show up in the midst of our follies and wanderings. In the storm and stress of a fractured relationship, God is there. In the shame and disgrace of failure, God is there. No matter where we try to go, God travels with us, continuing to pour out abundant grace and love. This grace doesn't go away.

Perhaps it's time to stop hiding; time to stop running. Maybe the moment has arrived to turn and accept God's incredible love and to allow the delusions to fall away. Could it be that the moment of transformation in God's loving grace is upon us?

Psalm 145:1-5, 17-21

The words of the ancient Sunday school teacher still ring clear in memory. "If you want to receive a blessing, you must be a blessing." These words have been a traveling partner for more than two decades of ministry, the words of this psalm conjure them up with fresh power.

The opening words are sung, perhaps danced with joy. "I will extol you my God and king and bless your name forever. Every day I will bless you...." And the psalm goes with the faithful blessing God because they themselves have been blessed. Who could take issue with such words? Who would even suggest that the faithful might not bless God? No one.

The unasked question here has to do with the shape and manner of said blessing. Does the psalm imply that we should dance, sing, and mouth our blessings all the day long? Does this writer imagine that the faithful should dress God with ever-more elaborate compliments? Perhaps so. But is that all?

No, it is not praise or elaborate liturgy that God desires. The prophet Amos makes this abundantly clear.

> *I hate, I despise your festivals,*
> *and I take no delight in your solemn assemblies.*
> *Even though you offer me your burnt offerings and grain*
> *offerings,*

I will not accept them;
*   and the offerings of well-being of your fatted animals*
*   I will not look upon.*
Take away from me the noise of your songs;
*   I will not listen to the melody of your harps.*
But let justice roll down like waters,
*   and righteousness like an ever-flowing stream.*
                                    — Amos 5:21-24

Indeed, the prophet stands in a critical pose as he reads through this psalm. It is a fitting stance for a prophet, and he does not stand alone. Isaiah and Micah stand, too, calling for an incarnation of blessing. These words accompany the psalmist through the centuries to our places of worship today.

How do the faithful bless God in this day and age? What shape do these blessings take? Are they merely the harmonies of hymns and songs or the intoned responses of prayers? Or are those songs accompanied by the rhythms of justice and peace? Do they walk on the earth as the music of liberation and the prayers of healing and disarmament?

If so, then perhaps that ancient Sunday school teacher's words were heard as we ourselves become the blessing we would offer our God.

Psalm 146

Many Christians can be heard in or out of worship these days as they lift up their voices and say, "Praise the Lord!" The phrases are familiar, almost rote. Mouths open and words emerge. Pastors and liturgists remind the faithful that this God is not only worthy of our praise; this God sort of requires it of us. This God is a jealous God (Exodus 20:5) who brooks no competition from other gods we might pursue. Yes, God is worthy of praise. Right?

After all, we are not in the habit of offering empty praise, are we? The boy who has done a good job raking the yard deserves praise. The worker who completes a task with excellent workmanship deserves praise. The spouse who is faithful over long years deserves praise. The question comes with halting hands raised from the back of the room. Yes, yes. We have heard it all before. God deserves our praise. But, if you don't mind the question, what has God done to be worthy of our praise?

The psalmist clears the throat and steps up to the plate with some answers. For starters, God made the universe, including us. Looking around, that seems pretty sufficient cause for praise. Yet that's not the end of the story. This psalm lists the reasons for praising God with stunning clarity. God is faithful. God gives justice to the oppressed. God feeds the hungry and sets the prisoners free. God opens the eyes of the blind and lifts up those who are bowed down. This God loves justice and watches over the strangers. This God looks out for the vulnerable ones in our midst.

If we deem a God who stands for such things as worthy of praise, then it stands to reason that we, too, should be standing for them. In fact, one could read this psalm as a call to partnership with God. Let us praise God with our voices, to be sure. But let our lives articulate the praise we have for this God who is the standard bearer for righteousness, this God who stands with those who are hurting, this God who calls us to be part of the juggernaut of justice.

What would such a partnership look like? How would we connect with the holy as we lift our hearts, voices, and lives in praise? What would our churches look like as they aligned their lives toward what could be labeled as "praise activism"? Let these questions stir hearts and stimulate conversation. Let the vision of partnership with the holy lead the church into a new day of praise and faithfulness.

And let the people live the words, "Praise the Lord!"

Psalm 146

There is a well-worn axiom that warns against mixing religion and politics. It was probably devised in an attempt to help smooth the rough places in some of those long holiday dinners with seldom-seen relatives. Keep the conversation polite, vague, and unchallenging. That way, all parties can stay through the dessert course and get home in one piece. In truth, there is wisdom in such an unwritten law. However, a serious people of faith must contend with the time after dinner when the relatives have dispersed and it's back to business as usual.

Such a moment arrives in the reading of Psalm 146. The psalm underscores a deep strain of the Judeo-Christian heritage that cannot be easily brushed aside. It is the plaintive call here to "not place our trust in princes or in mortals in whom there is no help." This is no stump speech for some brew of faith-based anarchy. It is not an attempt to overthrow established order. It is, simply put, a statement of obvious reality.

While all people are in need of good governance and reasonable processes for redress, the simple truth is that these systems and those who inhabit them are not to be trusted. A simple reading of history demonstrates this. Broken promises, shattered treaties, bloated bureaucracies, and rampant corruption riddle the governments of this world from Old Testament days right through to the moment of this writing.

The call comes to trust, instead, in God. It is God, we read, who executes justice, who liberates the oppressed, and gives sight to the blind. It is God who lifts up those who are bowed down and who loves the righteous. This is not an isolated notion within scripture. It's interesting to note that in this psalm can be found a thread that runs from here to Isaiah (58) to Jesus, who stands up in the temple in chapter 4 of Luke to announce the year of God's favor.

This thread wraps itself around the reality that all governments ultimately are the same in that they will all collapse and perish into vapors of history. What lasts, what stands, and what will always be with us is the powerful voice of our God. It is in this God we are called to place our trust. It is with this God we are called to walk. And it is this God, come to us in Christ Jesus, who calls us to lives that will create the year of God's favor now, in this day, and in this moment.

Psalm 146:5-10

In this season of waiting there is a prior question that comes to mind. Before the garlands are hung and wreaths are placed, before the Advent suppers and Christmas dinners, there is a question that twenty-first-century Christians sometimes overlook. While we're busy getting ready for the Savior to arrive, does anyone ask if we really want or need a Savior? Do we, in point of fact, need saving? If so, from what do we need saving?

With little fear of contradiction, let it be suggested that indeed we do need saving. If there's any doubt, this psalm offers us a list. We need to be saved from injustice, hunger, and oppression. We need to be saved from blindness and life's overwhelming burdens. The vulnerable among us also need saving. The stranger, the widow, and the orphan ... to mention only a few.

From this and more we need saving. In these days of waiting, it is this confession that may need to come before we decorate the sanctuary. Do we need saving? The answer is a firm, "Yes." Imagine a small group — a study group or a men's group — coming together over this psalm to consider the things from which "we" need saving — as individuals — as church community — as city or nation? From what can we all agree that we need God's intervention to save us?

Ah yes. God's intervention. Pastors, social workers, and mental health professionals sometimes get called in to do an "intervention." Frequently, such events involve an individual whose life is out of control. Often this loss of control is due to the abuse of alcohol or drugs, but whatever the reason, the slope is slippery and this person is in danger. In an intervention like this, the person's family, friends, and accompanying caregivers gather to intervene. The truth is told and hopefully the person is pulled out of denial and into a place where help can be offered.

Perhaps this is not a bad model to consider as we look to God's intervention. Are we a people out of control? Is hunger, deprivation, oppression, and violence rampant in our world? Are there other ways we are we out of control? From what do we need saving, and how might God's intervention be just what we need? With these questions considered in prayer and discernment, our season of preparation might just look a little different this year.

Psalm 147:1-11, 20c

Sometimes life gets to be simply too much. Virtually anyone can nod his or her head in weary agreement to this assertion. People work many more hours and handle more responsibilities than they did only a few years ago. Mention a forty-hour work week to most people, and a bemused smile comes back at you. Irony, it seems, isn't dead after all. Add to this the towering stack of personal and family obligations, community responsibilities, and financial commitments ... and it can cause someone to collapse under the collective weight of it all.

Clergy and health care professionals see this often in relatives who must care for family members in long-term illnesses. They see it, too, in single parenting situations where the demands of children and career stretch and pull a person to the tearing point. In fact, stress is almost a pandemic. It isn't that love goes away. It's simply that the burden can sometimes be more than even the strongest person can handle.

That's when it's good to collapse into a pew and give it all to God.

"How good it is to sing praises to our God!" (v. 1). How wonderful it is to release our cares and burdens in an avalanche of praise to one who can shoulder the things we cannot manage by ourselves. This God can bind up a broken heart (v. 3). This God can heal my wounds and lift me up when I've been beaten down by life's demands (v. 6). In fact, this God can do it all. From numbering the stars (v. 4), to casting down the wicked (v. 6b); from designing clouds, to feeding the livestock, this God has it together.

No matter how stressed or how tense we get. No matter how tightly wound our lives cause us to feel, there is one who is greater than it all. There is one who can take the burden and lighten the load.

Certainly the writer of this psalm didn't envision the chaos that makes up twenty-first-century life in America. But a

201

brokenhearted and wounded people were something that the writer probably did know firsthand. The one who crafted this psalm probably didn't have to cope with many of the complexities and stresses that assail people today, but a people who were stretched to the breaking point, the psalmist likely did understand from personal experience.

Yet in the end, then and now, it's still God who is in charge. Whether you are downtrodden by invaders and held in exile, or imprisoned in stress-laden work that can, in fact, kill you, God is still God ... creator, covenant partner, healer, liberator ... God.

How good it is indeed to give praise to God!

Psalm 148

Into everyone's life comes a moment of complete abandonment of all the careful boundaries and filters we have put into place. For each person there is a moment of wild joy and unrestricted passion.

For us as a people of faith, these moments come as we abandon ourselves to unqualified praise of the almighty God. In some of our traditions, such abandonment causes discomfort. Passion is not easily controlled. But then, neither is the Holy Spirit.

It is this kind of wild praise that can be felt in this psalm. The call is clear and unambiguous. Praise the Lord! Everyone and everything is called upon to shout out the glory of the creating God! From sea monsters to the elements to topography and back again; all are called upon to enter into the dance of praise.

It is easy to imagine Saint Francis shouting out the words to this psalm as he danced through the forest and claimed a life of simple service and poverty. It is a little less easy to imagine one's pastor in such a paroxysm of praise. It is still harder to imagine oneself stomping and shouting out praises to God.

Yet, it is the call, not merely of this psalm, but of our faith.

God, after all, is God. The great "I AM" (Exodus 3:14). This is the creator God, the one who brings us redemption through (his Son) on this Christmas Day. This is the God who knows each person down to the number of hairs on the scalp. This is the God who loves each one of us just as we are.

If all this is true, which we claim today that it is, how can we do anything but jump and shout our praises? How can there be any other response than this? Let all creation issue forth a chorus of wonder and joy, a cacophony of celebration. How blessed and fortunate we are! For God has done great things for us and given us a Savior, born this day in Bethlehem. And his name is called Jesus.

What else can we do but sing our praises?

What other choice do we have but to set aside our puny agendas and complicated tasks and simply shout to the heavens, "PRAISE THE LORD!"

Psalm 148

Enthusiasm is not in vogue these days. Just about anywhere one chooses to look, the contemporary emotional trend is what might be called a vague detachment. Think about it. How many people are excited about government today? Even those in power will readily point out that government's a bad thing that should really not get involved in peoples' lives. This reflection is being written, of course, as more and more cameras are mounted on every street corner in America. How many people are enthusiastic about their jobs? With corporate America replacing job security with pink slips in the incessant drive for ever higher profits, who can blame them? Enthusiasm? They're lucky to have a job. How many people are enthusiastic about their families? With families across the land split and broken, enthusiasm for relationships can run low indeed. Does it seem that many are enthusiastic about life in general? No, rather we practice an aloof indifference and look down our noses at those who engage in unseemly enthusiasm.

The reason for this attitude problem is anyone's guess. Perhaps former Education Secretary Richard Riley got it right when he said, "We are victims of the tyranny of lowered expectations." Maybe it's a way to avoid commitment — and therefore any possibility of discomfort due to failure. After all, you can't fail if you don't try, right? It's anyone's guess really. But there's no doubt about it. From teenagers to retirees and back again, we are awash in cynicism and a decided lack of enthusiasm.

Yet, enthusiasm is exactly what faith calls us to practice. Faith bids us to pull out all the stops and "praise the Lord from the highest heavens!" Praise presupposes enthusiasm. Praising God without enthusiasm really isn't praise at all, is it? Imagine a room full of people slouched over in the body language of detachment, mumbling the words to this psalm. It's almost a comical image, yet how many of us have seen exactly this in youth group meetings and worship services over the years? It's as if the unspoken message is, "I'm here, aren't I? Isn't that enough?"

No, actually, it's not enough. We are recipients of a sacred call to drop our jaded attitudes and break out in unrestrained shouts of praise! No middle ground here. No downcast eyes and bent shoulders. No slipping quietly into the background. Look around and see what God has wrought! Cast a glance into the distance and see the utter glory of creation! Then focus the eye a little closer to home. Lift a finger. Look at it. The marvelous "handiwork" of muscle, tissue, and bone, all knit together with the craftsmanship of the master.

There's no mediocrity here. Only excellence; the same kind of excellence to which God calls us as we step into the new year. So let there be no mumbling or slouching. Sing in the streets! Dance on the freeways! From angels, to moon and stars, to sea monsters and beyond! Let all things their creator bless! Praise the Lord!

Psalm 148

What better way to begin a new year than with unqualified praise for our God! As the minutes of the old year tick quickly by and we contemplate a new beginning in the form of a new year, it is an appropriate time to stop and drop everything as we give all of our praise to God. What better way to give praise than to pray this psalm together?

New Year's resolutions are a great thing. Making a vow to be a better parent or spouse, promising to do better at work, pledging to be a more faithful church member, resolving to lose those few extra pounds, all these are good.

Before we step into it all, let's lay the foundation of praise.

In this psalm, the poetry of God's wonder is a riot of images and glory. We are called in an almost sacred recklessness to list out God's wonderful doings. God commanded it was created! God set the limits and boundaries ... and expects us to observe them. All creation, according to this psalm, praises the Lord. And what better grounding for the beginning of a new year?

If we begin with praise, everything else comes a little differently. If our relationships, our work, our fulfillment of duties are begun in an aura of praising God, imagine how things might be different.

Praising God for the gift of children, for example, will have an impact on how we parent and guide them. Praising God for the gift of productive work will flavor the way we approach our jobs. Giving thanks, even, for the difficulties and challenges that come our way will shape the ways in which we respond to these things.

Laying a foundation of praise is not an easy thing to do, but it will make a difference in the lives we lead in the New Year. Just as the foundation of a house is laid out before the carpenters and framers come into the picture, so, too, do we lay out the foundation of praise.

The foundation stones here are those of thankful prayer and focusing upon God. How many times a day do we stop and simply say, whatever our situation, "Thank you, God"? To some, such focus might seem immature or even silly. But it is the stuff of new life. Read this psalm over several times. Breathe in the air of praise that comes from the powerful language. Imagine how you might utter a psalm of praise. Indeed, grab a pen and sit down and write one!

Whatever our hopes and dreams for this New Year might be, there is a call to us to found these visions and aspirations upon grateful hearts rooted in God's love.

Happy New Year.

Psalm 148

Most people spend their lives hungering after praise. Children thirst for it from parents, family, teachers, and friends. Young adults warm to its glow as they take on professional responsibilities and enter into adult relationships. As the midlife years approach, men and women are nourished by praise that comes as a result of committed and long-term relationships. Even in old age, praise continues to matter a great deal. Many people, of course, learn to live without praise, but it's a bleak existence.

People need affirmation and uplifting care. Counselors and mental health professionals will attest to this. Without praise, the spirit withers and the heart contracts. Without the wind of appreciation flowing under life's wings, it's hard to fly; difficult to soar. People who live their lives without praise tend to be cold, distant, and lifeless. The reason is that praise, simply put, is life-giving. It is the water that soaks into the roots of our souls causing us to blossom and grow.

Thinking about how praise operates within human community makes for interesting fodder when it is time to give praise to God. Today's psalm reverberates with the joy of this praise. It resonates with wonder and bursts the restraints of normal expression with shouts that are both urgent and loving. "Praise the Lord!" comes, in this instance, almost as a command. Everyone and everything should echo God's praise, and they should do it now!

Yes, of course God should be praised. Few seriously challenge this notion. But the question comes as to whether we praise God because of God's need ... or because of our own need. Can it be that the creator of the universe needs affirmation and praise in the same way that human beings have need of it? Or does the sound of our singing and prayer emerge from our own need to surrender to that which is greater than ourselves?

The temptation to create God in our image is virtually irresistible. Scriptures are full of such mirrored images, and it is an understandable misstep. As humans, we inevitably translate the world through our own experience. But it's important to recall that the reality is exactly the opposite of our own feeble efforts. God created human beings in God's image; not the other way around.

It is likely that God has little need of our praise. Human beings, on the other hand, have a deep need to give themselves in
worship and service to their creator. So it is that we lift up our
voices with this powerful psalm: "Praise the Lord!"

Psalm 149

The very words, "Praise the Lord," have, in some circles, taken
on a tone of mockery and scorn. In certain quarters, one can hear
the high nasal satiric voice as it bleats out the opening words to
this psalm. "Praaaise the Lorrrrd!" It's true. Making fun of Christian faith is quite fashionable these days. From comedians to
songwriters to self-proclaimed spiritual-but-not-religious folk, a
steady stream of ridicule flows unabated.

The taunting disrespect comes for a lot of reasons. It is aimed
at hypocritical television preachers who are quick to judge the moral
turpitude of others, only to themselves be found severely wanting.
It is leveled at religious institutions that are far more engaged in
the maintenance of the institution than in actually praising the Lord.
Yes, the mockery comes from many places, but it is generated by
what the world clearly sees as a religious community unable to
live up to its own teachings.

Maybe, as this psalm suggests, it's time to sing a "new song."
Perhaps this song brings with it the melody of humility, tolerance,
and hope. How does it go? Could there be harmonies of forgiveness, grace, and openness? What's the beat? Is it the rhythm of
generosity and peace? Does it have a backbeat of compassion and
justice?

There's no question about it. Listening to the rising tide of
critique and outright condemnation of Christian faith raises the
hackles. Yet, if honesty prevails, it must be admitted that much of
the negative energy directed at the Christian community is richly
deserved. We have not lived by the teachings of Jesus. We have not
stood up for the poor and the weak. We are not good at loving our
enemies, and we do not make a real great showing at offering forgiveness. We have uttered empty, pious judgments and held to le-
galistic rulings while grace has been discarded and left behind.

And we have looked the other way while people waving the cross of Christ have used his name for economic and political gain.

Yes, indeed. It is time to sing a new song. Let the song come, but not as a way to stem the tide of criticism. Let it come instead as a true and powerful symphony of praise to the holy creating God of Israel! Let this new song call the "assembly" to faithfulness and the leaders to integrity and passion. Let the notes of new life pour forth as the whole community joins with one voice to sing a new song.

Psalm 149

Within the confines of our cultural reality, those who take things into their own hands are showered with praise. Words like, "initiative," and "take charge," describe those who get ahead. But for the faithful of Israel, and thus for those claiming Judeo-Christian roots in this moment, God is the one who is in charge. Not us, not our kings or leaders, but God.

This psalm articulates this awareness as Israel celebrates God's power with rejoicing and with music. The language is beautiful but could be misunderstood as a nod to holy warriors and such. The praise of God is in their throats, and the two-edged sword is indeed held high. But the words and the weapons wait upon God. An old cliché comes to mind that describes the sense of this psalm extremely well. "Work as though everything depends upon you, and pray with the knowledge that everything depends upon God."

It turns out that it's not the aggressive or the initiative-takers who win in the end. It's God's humble and faithful followers who wait upon God's will, rather than their own agenda. The question comes about today's faithful and the willingness to abandon agenda and initiative to wait upon God's will and direction. What would happen if pastors and leaders did that in churches today? The ready answer is that nothing would happen. Things would drift, and the people would be directionless. But is that really true?

For those who depend upon God, hard work can never be abandoned. Striving and struggle are part of God's plan. The important thing, however, is not the doing, but the focus upon doing God's will rather than our own.

Herein lies the day-to-day struggle all people of faith face. Each moment, each action, each word must be accompanied by the perpetual question. Is this about me ... or about God? Is this project about my ego and sense of accomplishment? Or is it about advancing the community, the kingdom of God? Are the words about to be spoken by me, words that build up God's purpose or my own? Call it discernment. Call it prayer. Call it spiritual attentiveness or whatever name can be summoned up, but it is a key process in faithful living.

This is the victory that comes to the humble. This is the glory exalted by the faithful. It is the joy that bubbles forth from the couches and from the pews.

1 Samuel 2:1-10

Comparisons are something we humans seem unable to avoid. Shakespeare, in his famed sonnet, was looking for something to compare to the fairness of his love. Of course, in the biblical texts, the Song of Solomon also seeks to compare the lover to a series of enticing images. But it's more than lovers that fall under the eye of human comparison. We compare virtually everything: from children to spouses to jobs to cars and beyond, we are always comparing.

The truth is that we need comparisons. How would the contrast and comparison of the things we experience in life make people find good careers if they did not compare jobs? In what ways would people choose husbands or wives if they had not dated and had some standard to compare? If someone has a favorite food, how do they know it is the favorite? They know by means of contrast and comparison.

At first glance, Hannah's prayer seems to have the same need of comparison when it comes to God. Who is like God? Who is seated on high? Who looks down on the heavens and the earth? Think for a moment. While we are certainly capable of choosing to go after other gods, the writer of this psalm doesn't seem to be seeking a contrast and comparison between an array of competing gods. Instead, the writer uses the guise of comparison to make a superlative statement and dares anyone to try to compare with the wonders of God.

The point is well made. Though we might chase after the gods of money, power, or control, it is clear in the end that there simply is no comparison. Though we might elevate certain leaders or ideas to godlike levels, once again we must concede that there really is no comparison when it comes to the God of Israel.

God is God — our creator, redeemer, and sustainer, and there is none like God. The glove is on the ground. The challenge is made. "Go ahead," says our psalm, "I dare you to find anything that is like this wonderful, holy, and mighty God." While many try, none will ever even come close enough to make comparison a thing to be taken seriously.

So we join this joyful spirit of clarity in prayer and praise to utter those words we hear so often. "Praise the Lord!"

Isaiah 12:2-6

After a long and grueling foot race, a runner reached for a glass of water puffing out the words, "This water is my salvation!" A worker who had a family crisis gushed to a friend who agreed to cover his shift, "You are my salvation!" The drunk at the end of the bar lifts the shot glass to his lips and sighs into the drink, "You are my salvation."

We often think of many things or people as saving us. But as the illustrations show, we sometimes trivialize, if not demean, the idea of salvation. Other times we are capable of giving substance to the idea. The heroic firefighter who pulls a little girl from a burning building, the research scientist who develops a vaccine, the friend who accepts a blow for another, there are indeed a million different ways in which people save one another.

These kinds of saving echo the salvation that we find in God. The "water that we draw from the well of salvation" is the water of a special kind of love. It is the saving love of a God who created and loves us. It is the healing love of a God who would bind us up and heal us.

When we lean into God's salvation, we lean away from fear and into trust. When we place God at the center of our lives as our salvation, we ourselves become capable of saving.

Such a statement may lead some to think that we are placing ourselves on a par with God. Not so. But it *is* true that Jesus called us to greater things than he did (John 14:12). Surely, our salvation is in God and God alone. Yet, if we have found that salvation, we will be changed into ones who offer that self-same saving love to others. This is what Paul writes about in Romans 12 when he calls upon the church not to be conformed to this world, but "transformed."

Those who have found their salvation in God are indeed transformed. They are a "new creation" (2 Corinthians 5:17). And as people transformed by God's love we, too, will begin to share that transformation life. This is a holy partnership. This is the call to those who wait upon the coming of the Messiah. Yes, indeed, a mighty one is coming, but this Savior does not intend to leave us as we are.

Luke 1:47-55

A common gift to young children is a magnifying glass. At first, the kids look at pieces of bread or spots on the floor. They peer into each other's eyes and look at their skin, all in a kind of awe at the way the world can look differently through this piece of glass. Then, inevitably, they come to find that they can hold this glass in the sunlight and it is capable of burning things! At first, it's just little pieces of wood, but then temptation enters the picture and all kinds of things — and even creatures — fall victim to the unchecked childish use of the magnifying glass.

It turns out that our souls are much like the magnifying glass. Our souls can magnify almost anything we choose. In a confrontation or crisis, one's soul can magnify anger or vengeance. When tragedy befalls us, our souls can magnify grief, confusion, and pain. In the face of injustice, our souls can magnify what we think is righteous anger. What things, over our lives, have our souls magnified? It is a moment of self-reflection worth taking, because the truth is that we get to choose what our souls magnify.

In Mary's case, she isn't just making a passing statement. She has made a choice. She says with fervor and deep, deep commitment, "*My* soul magnifies the Lord." Of all the choices before me or all the things I could do with my soul, I choose for it to magnify the Lord!

Indeed, much of scripture is laid out for us in the context of choices such as this. When we say the Lord's Prayer every Sunday, few realize that a choice is being articulated. "Our Father, who art in heaven, hallowed be *thy* name...." In praying this prayer, a choice is made, a destiny set, a pathway taken. Of all the things, names, and would-be gods, we choose to hallow the name of the God of Israel, the God of Jacob, the Abba, or Father of our Lord Jesus Christ.

Tonight, as we gather at the stable door, let us — with Mary — make the choice. In this birthing hour, and in the hours and days to come, may our souls magnify the Lord!

Luke 1:68-79

Jesus has many names. Even a brief pause to imagine it conjures up an ever-lengthening list. The task would be an interesting one, but not our focus just now. The one particular name for Jesus that comes to mind in this Advent time is "Prince of Peace." Taken from Isaiah's prophecy (Isaiah 9:6), this name heralds one who can and will lead us to peace, if only we would let him. Into a world fractured with the horrors of war, this baby Jesus comes to "guide our feet into the way of peace," as the prophecy of Zechariah puts it. But the real question is, will we let ourselves be guided?

Accompanying this "mighty Savior" that is to be raised up for us, is our own stupidity as a people. God may be looking favorably on us in this season, but we ourselves are blinded by the blood of the innocents. How can we embrace the peace that Christ brings when we are busy tearing one another apart in countless spots around the globe?

Oh, yes. Some say that war is horrible, but sometimes necessary. Jesus says, "Love your enemy" (Matthew 5:43). Some say that we have to protect our interests and save ourselves. Jesus says you have to lose your life to gain new life in him (Luke 9:24). Some say that God is on their side as the bodies pile up in dreadful counting. But God is only on the side of life, wanting it in abundance for all people (John 10:10).

There is no getting around it. Violence and warfare is contrary to the mind of Christ and the will of God. In this Advent time, the people who wear the name of Christ are called, indeed are challenged, to allow them to be guided into the way of peace. Allowing ourselves to be guided means that we must give up the delusion that we are leading. We must stop and allow God's love in Christ Jesus to lead us. Allowing ourselves to be guided means that we don't necessarily have all the answers. We need to be open to the leading of the Spirit. Allowing ourselves to be guided also means that we let go of our own ideas of the ultimate destination.

There is an old spiritual that comes to mind regarding all this:

> *Guide my feet Lord, while I run this race ...*
> *For I don't want to run this race in vain ...*

The song reveals a powerful truth. It is the fact that if we don't "allow" God to guide our steps, it is altogether likely that the race, our lives, will be led in vain.

Luke 1:68-79

Known among scholars as the "Benedictus," Zechariah's prophecy is a powerful and beautiful commentary on what is about to take place. The coming of the Messiah is recounted here in an incredible merger of spiritual, social, and political realities. The people will be delivered from their enemies, and they will gain knowledge of salvation. The sins of the people will be forgiven by God's tender mercies as the light of a new dawn guides "our feet into the way of peace."

What stunning imagery is here. What a powerful description of a new reality rooted in the coming of the Messiah. These few words sculpt a graphic vision of this reality, which is still available to present-day Christians.

It is a reality described by Jesus when in some frustration he exclaimed, "The kingdom of God is not coming with signs to be observed; nor will they say, 'Lo, here it is!' or 'There!' for behold, the kingdom of God is in the midst of you" (Luke 17:20-21).

Truly, the kingdom of God is in our midst. It is not a place, a political agenda, or a doctrinal list to which the faithful must assent. It is a totally new reality brought to us by God in Christ Jesus. The dawn (v. 78) has broken upon us. The light has come to "those who sit in the darkness and in the shadow of death," and it has come to "guide our feet into the way of peace."

Now comes the task of living into this reality of kingdom. The knowledge of salvation is ours. The pathway to peace is lit. The challenge now, is not to wait idly for some future event, but instead to live boldly and joyfully into the present reality of the kingdom of God. This is a reality where sins are forgiven, where the hungry are fed, and the homeless are housed. It is a present process where the people engage in the building of justice and the making of peace.

This prophecy of Zechariah has been realized. The Messiah has come. The kingdom is, as scripture tells us, "near" to us. Now it is our turn. We, the faithful and we, the ones who have faith, must dare to lean into this reality. The trick is to take the risk of living in this moment as though it were all true. The hope is for Christian communities everywhere to become islands where this reality, this kingdom is built, strengthened, and nurtured. "Blessed be the Lord God of Israel, for (he) has looked favorably upon his people and redeemed them."

Today is the day to embrace this redemption, to receive, and to live in the kingdom.

About The Author

The Reverend Schuyler Rhodes is celebrating the beginning of his tenth year as the pastor of Temple United Methodist Church in San Francisco, California.

He received his Bachelor of Arts degree from the State University of New York at Potsdam and his Master of Divinity with honors from Drew University in Madison, New Jersey. Pastor Rhodes has also carried on graduate studies in Literature and Criticism at State University of New York at Albany and in Liberation at Maryknoll School of Theology.

He has served churches in New York City, New Jersey, and in rural New York State. His other experiences include Campus Ministry, Retreat Director, Teacher and Workshop Leader, and serving as the National Director for Peace with Justice Week. Schuyler has had extensive public speaking experience, traveling throughout Europe and the United States. He has also served as Consultant on Peace and Justice Ministries to the General Board of Global Ministries Women's Division, and served for nine years as President of the Board of Directors of the Interreligious Foundation for Community Organization.

Pastor Rhodes serves on the Board of Directors of the California Council of Churches and the San Francisco United Methodist Mission. He sits on the Steering Committee of the Religious Witness with Homeless People and the Advisory Board of the National Equal Justice Association. He is also deeply involved in the ministry of his denomination, the United Methodist Church, where he holds a number of ministry responsibilities beyond the local church.

An accomplished author, Reverend Rhodes has published numerous articles and monographs as well as four books

- *Words of Hope and Clarity* (CSS Publishing Company)
- *Words for a Birthing Church* (CSS Publishing Company)
- *Pentecost Fire: Preaching Hope in Times of Change* (CSS Publishing Company)

- *Words to the Silence: A Book of Uncommon Prayer* (Educational Ministries Press, Prescott, Arizona)

He is married to Lisa Quoresimo and is the father of Emma Elizabeth and Aaron Schuyler, both age fourteen. His spare-time interests involve a love of music. Schuyler plays guitar and mandolin and enjoys playing in a musical collaboration called Canaan Roads, with whom he recently recorded a CD. He also loves spending time at the family's mountain retreat in the Sierra Nevada foothills, where he writes and spends time working outdoors.

Psalms In The Revised Common Lectionary
Index II Format

Psalm	Occasion	Year
Ps 1	Epiphany 6 [6]	C
Ps 1	Easter 7	B
Ps 1+	Proper 20 [25]	B
Ps 1*	Proper 18 [23]	C
Ps 1*	Proper 25 [30]	A
Ps 2 (Alt)	Epiphany Last Transfig.	A
Ps 4	Easter 3	B
Ps 5:1-8+	Proper 6 [11]	C
Ps 8	Trinity Sunday	AC
Ps 8	New Year	ABC
Ps 8*	Proper 22 [27]	B
Ps 9:9-20 (Alt)+	Proper 7 [12]	B
Ps 13+	Proper 8 [13]	A
Ps 14+	Proper 12 [17]	B
Ps 14+	Proper 19 [24]	C
Ps 15	Epiphany 4 [4]	A
Ps 15*	Proper 17 [22]	B
Ps 15*	Proper 11 [16]	C
Ps 16	Easter 2	A
Ps 16*	Proper 28 [33]	B
Ps 16*	Proper 8 [13]	C
Ps 17:1-7, 15+	Proper 13 [18]	A
Ps 17:1-9*	Proper 27 [32]	C
Ps 19	Lent 3	B
Ps 19	Epiphany 3 [3]	C
Ps 19+	Proper 22 [27]	A
Ps 19 (Alt)+	Proper 19 [24]	B
Ps 19:7-14*	Proper 21 [26]	B
Ps 20+	Proper 6 [11]	B
Ps 22	Good Friday	ABC
Ps 22:1-15+	Proper 23 [28]	B
Ps 22:19-28	Proper 7 [12]	C
Ps 22:23-31	Lent 2	B
Ps 22:25-31	Easter 5	B
Ps 23	Easter 4	ABC
Ps 23	Lent 4	A
Ps 23*	Proper 23 [28]	A
Ps 23*	Proper 11 [16]	B
Ps 24	All Saints	B
Ps 24+	Proper 10 [15]	B
Ps 25:1-9*	Proper 21 [26]	A
Ps 25:1-10	Lent 1	B
Ps 25:1-10	Advent 1	C
Ps 25:1-10*	Proper 10 [15]	C
Ps 26+	Proper 22 [27]	B
Ps 26:1-8*	Proper 17 [22]	A
Ps 27	Lent 2	C
Ps 27:1, 4-9	Epiphany 3 [3]	A
Ps 29	Baptism of the Lord [1]	ABC
Ps 29	Trinity Sunday	B
Ps 30	Epiphany 6 [6]	B
Ps 30	Easter 3	C
Ps 30+	Proper 9 [14]	C
Ps 30*	Proper 5 [10]	C
Ps 30*	Proper 8 [13]	B
Ps 31:1-5, 19-24*	Proper 4 [9]	A
Ps 31:9-16	Palm/Passion Sunday	ABC
Ps 31:1-5, 15-16	Easter 5	A
Ps 32	Lent 1	A
Ps 32	Lent 4	C
Ps 32*	Proper 6 [11]	C
Ps 32:1-7*	Proper 26 [31]	C
Ps 33:1-12+	Proper 5 [10]	A
Ps 33:12-22*	Proper 14 [19]	C
Ps 34:1-8, (19-22)+	Proper 25 [30]	B
Ps 34:1-8*	Proper 14 [19]	B
Ps 34:1-10, 22	All Saints	A
Ps 34:9-14*	Proper 15 [20]	B
Ps 34:15-22*	Proper 16 [21]	B
Ps 36:5-10	Epiphany 2 [2]	C
Ps 37:1-9*	Epiphany 7 [7]	C
Ps 37:1-11, 39-40		
Ps 40:1-11	Epiphany 2 [2]	A
Ps 41	Epiphany 7 [7]	B
Pss 42 and 43	Proper 7 [12]	C
Ps 43*	Proper 26 [31]	A
Ps 45:10-17+	Proper 9 [14]	A

218

Ps 95	Lent 3	A
Ps 95:1-7a	Proper 29 [34]	A
Ps 96	Christmas Day 1	ABC
Ps 96+	Proper 4 [9]	C
Ps 96:1-9, (10-13)*	Proper 24 [29]	A
Ps 96:1-9	Epiphany 9 [9]	C
Ps 96:1-9*	Proper 4 [9]	C
Ps 97	Christmas Day 2	ABC
Ps 97	Easter 7	C
Ps 98	Christmas Day 3	ABC
Ps 98	Easter 6	B
Ps 98+	Proper 27 [32]	C
Ps 98*	Proper 28 [33]	C
Ps 99+	Proper 24 [29]	A
Ps 99	Epiphany Last Transfig.	AC
Ps 100*	Proper 6 [11]	A
Ps 100	Reign of Christ [34]	A
Ps 100+	Thanksgiving	C
Ps 103:(1-7), 8-13*	Proper 19 [24]	A
Ps 103:1-8	Proper 16 [21]	C
Ps 103:1-13, 22	Epiphany 8 [8]	B
Ps 104:1-9, 24, 35c+	Proper 24 [29]	B
Ps 104:24-34, 35b	Pentecost	ABC
Ps 105:1-6, 16-22 45b+	Proper 14 [19]	A
Ps 105:1-6, 37-45+	Proper 20 [25]	A
Ps 105:1-6, 23-26, 45c+	Proper 17 [22]	A
Ps 105:1-11, 45b+ (Alt)	Proper 12 [17]	A
Ps 106:1-6, 19-23+	Proper 23 [28]	A
Ps 107:1-3, 17-22	Lent 4	B
Ps 107:1-3, 23-32*	Proper 7 [12]	B
Ps 107:1-7, 33-37+	Proper 26 [31]	A
Ps 107:1-9, 43+	Proper 13 [18]	C
Ps 110	Ascension	C
Ps 111	Epiphany 4 [4]	B
Ps 111+	Proper 15 [20]	B
Ps 111*	Proper 23 [28]	C
Ps 112*	Proper 17 [22]	C
Ps 112:1-9 (10)	Epiphany 5 [5]	A
Ps 113*	Proper 20 [25]	C
Ps 114	Easter Vigil	ABC
Ps 114	Easter Evening	ABC
Ps 114 (Alt)+	Proper 19 [24]	A
Ps 116:1-4, 12-19	Easter 3	A
Ps 116:1-2, 12-19+	Proper 6 [11]	A
Ps 116:1-2, 12-19	Holy Thursday	ABC
Ps 116:1-9*	Proper 19 [24]	B
Ps 118:1-2, 14-24	Easter	ABC
Ps 118:1-2, 19-29 (palms)	Palm/Passion Sunday	ABC
Ps 118:14-29 (Alt)	Easter 2	C
Ps 119:1-8	Epiphany 6 [6]	A
Ps 119:1-8*	Proper 26 [31]	B
Ps 119:9-16 (Alt)	Lent 5	B
Ps 119:33-40	Epiphany 7 [7]	A
Ps 119:33-40*	Proper 18 [23]	A
Ps 119:97-104+	Proper 24 [29]	C
Ps 119:105-112+	Proper 10 [15]	A
Ps 119:129-136*	Proper 12 [17]	A
Ps 119:137-144+	Proper 26 [31]	C
Ps 121	Lent 2	A
Ps 121*	Proper 24 [29]	C
Ps 122	Advent 1	A
Ps 123+	Proper 28 [33]	A
Ps 123*	Proper 9 [14]	B
Ps 124+	Proper 16 [21]	A
Ps 124+	Proper 21 [26]	B

Ps 125+	Proper 18 [23]	B
Ps 126 (Alt)	Advent 3	B
Ps 126*	Proper 25 [30]	B
Ps 126	Thanksgiving	B
Ps 126	Lent 5	C
Ps 127+	Proper 27 [32]	B
Ps 128+	Proper 12 [17]	A
Ps 130	Lent 5	A
Ps 130+	Proper 8 [13]	B
Ps 130+	Proper 14 [19]	B
Ps 130*	Proper 5 [10]	B
Ps 131	Epiphany 8 [8]	A
Ps 132:1-12, (13-18)+	Reign of Christ [34]	B
Ps 133+	Proper 15 [20]	A
Ps 133 (Alt)+	Proper 7 [12]	B
Ps 133	Easter 2	B
Ps 137 (Alt)+	Proper 22 [27]	C
Ps 138*	Proper 16 [21]	A
Ps 138+	Proper 5 [10]	B
Ps 138*	Proper 12 [17]	C
Ps 138	Epiphany 5 [5]	C
Ps 139:1-6, 13-18	Epiphany 2 [2]	B
Ps 139:1-6, 13-18+	Proper 4 [9]	B
Ps 139:1-6, 13-18+	Proper 18 [23]	C
Ps 139:1-12, 23-24+	Proper 11 [16]	A
Ps 145:1-8*	Proper 20 [25]	A
Ps 145:8-9, 14-21*	Proper 13 [18]	A
Ps 145:8-14*	Proper 9 [14]	A
Ps 145:10-18*	Proper 12 [17]	B
Ps 145:1-5, 17-21 (Alt)+	Proper 27 [32]	C
Ps 146:5-10 (Alt)	Advent 3	A
Ps 146*	Proper 27 [32]	B
Ps 146*	Proper 18 [23]	B
Ps 146*	Proper 21 [26]	C
Ps 146+	Proper 26 [31]	B
Ps 146+	Proper 5 [10]	C
Ps 147:1-11, 20c	Epiphany 5 [5]	B
Ps 147:12-20 (Alt)	Christmas 2	ABC
Ps 148	Christmas 1	ABC
Ps 148	Easter 5	C
Ps 149+	Proper 18 [23]	A
Ps 149	All Saints	C
Ps 150	Easter 2	C

CPSIA information can be obtained
at www.ICGtesting.com
Printed in the USA
BVHW042141170519
548587BV00001B/43/P